Take Five!

Staying Alert at Home and School

Mary Sue Williams
Sherry Shellenberger

Published by
TherapyWorks, Inc.
Albuquerque, NM
toll free 1.877.897.3478
505.899.4071 (fax)
www.AlertProgram.com

First printing: 2001
Reprinted: Five Times
Seventh Printing: February 2011

How Does Your Engine Run?® and *Alert Program*® are trademarks of TherapyWorks, Inc.

Use with proper supervision.

ISBN #978-0-9643041-1-6

ACKNOWLEDGEMENTS

We would like to acknowledge gratefully all who have supported us in this writing. Many friends and colleagues helped to bolster us through the writing process and celebrate the final product. We could not have done it without them! We deeply appreciate each and every one of their special ways of giving to the project:

Graphic Designer and Illustrator:
Laura Reed

Editor:
Betsy Noll

Occupational Therapy Coach and Mentor:
Patti Oetter

Reviewers:
George Bach, Joanne Bach, Laura Barker, Stacie Bunch, Judy DeWalch, Martha Gomez, Sandey Guidice, Mary Hooper, Sarah Masur, Patti Oetter, Yvonne Randall, Kim Samelstad, Julie Wilbarger, Melissa Winkle, Kris Worrel, and Carla Cay Williams.

And all the others who supported us in numerous ways:
Anne Arkon, Sharon Azar, Paulette Christopher, Meg Colby, Meg Cox, Rebecca Jo Dakota, Liz Davenport, Jane Einhorn, Bob Gaines, Willi Harms, Irene Henio, Anne Hubbard, Mary Houdek, Laurie Haase, Marci Laurel, Millie Leahy, Havens Levitt, Jacqui Lewnes, Kris Michalko, Mike Michalko, Judy Reisman, Eileen Richter, Steve Richter, Gabe Tovar, Maryann Trott, Cheryl Travers, Norma Vasquez, Dave Williams, Ron Winkle, and our canine writing buddies, Boomer and Norina.

DEDICATION

To June Reed, Irene Henio, and all the teachers,
therapists, parents, and students
in the Gallup-McKinley County Schools
for our years together
where we learned the most about "Taking Five!"

ABOUT THE AUTHORS ————

Mary Sue Williams and Sherry Shellenberger, both occupational therapists, have over 25 years of experience working with and learning from a variety of children, parents, and teachers in urban and rural school districts as well as clinic, home, and camp settings. They have focused on developing practical ways to teach people of all ages how to incorporate sensory processing theory into every day living. Since 1987, they have developed, refined, and "kid-tested" the Alert Program®. One of their greatest joys is watching children (and their adults) find the answers to the question, "How does your engine run?"

As co-owners of TherapyWorks, Inc., Mary Sue and Sherry have self-published products relating to self-regulation including their Leader's Guide book, *"How Does Your Engine Run?"® A Leader's Guide to the Alert Program® for Self-Regulation*, their Introductory Booklet, *An Introduction to "How Does Your Engine Run?" The Alert Program for Self-Regulation*, and their double CD set, *The Alert Program: Songs for Self-Regulation*. In addition, they offer the simplest way to teach about self-regulation in the book/CD, *Test Drive: Introducing the Alert Program through Song.*

Since 1991, thousands of professionals have attended Alert Program trainings with enthusiastic reviews. Recently, they decided to lecture full-time to "spread the word" about how using the engine analogy and understanding self-regulation can enrich the lives of children. Since children are their finest teachers, Sherry and Mary Sue now enjoy volunteering time in the Albuquerque community where they look forward to learning more from their "instructors."

Leisure time activities? Even with her busy schedule, Sherry finds time to play tennis, read mysteries, scuba dive, and "joke around." Mary Sue enjoys cooking, camping, watching sunsets, and spending time with her dog friends, as they learn to be service dogs.

TABLE OF CONTENTS

One

The "Take Five!" Concepts

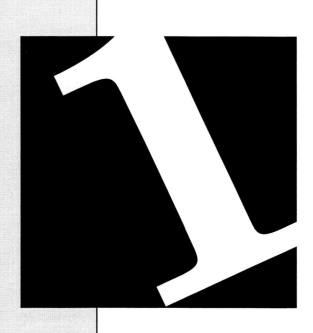

The "Take Five" Concepts

Take Five! is a compilation of years of working with and learning from children, families, school staff, and the thousands of participants who have attended our **"How Does Your Engine Run?"**® conferences. This book is intended for all who want to help children to learn. Our hope is that parents, teachers, therapists, and especially children will benefit by using these activities and ideas in homes and schools.

In our culture that is increasingly fast-paced, high-tech, and more sedentary, we all need to remember to "take five." Our bodies and brains are not built to sit for hour after hour at computers, in meetings, or in classrooms. We've all had the experience of facing a deadline and needing to finish a project. No matter how good our intentions, there comes a moment when we "hit the wall." We are no longer as efficient, capable, motivated, or perhaps even safe in completing the task. We feel eye strain, tension in our muscles, and we know fatigue is setting in. We feel our concentration waning. The brain and body beg us to take a break. Unfortunately, we often ignore these signals and think we can finish the project more quickly if we just push ourselves. Yet, if we "take five," we often will gain more . . . more in our ability to attend, to focus, to concentrate and even to avoid injuries (e.g., repetitive stress injuries to wrists, backs, and necks). By taking a break, we can often gain 20 minutes, 30 minutes, or perhaps an hour of productive time. In this book, we will share a wide-range of suggestions and activities to support optimal alertness. We hope that all (typically and atypically developing children, as well as adults) will find that this book helps them complete that next project with less effort and more efficiency.

The concepts and activities in this book have been "kid-tested" and "adult-approved" for over a decade. *Take Five!* provides the practical know-how and an extensive list of activities from which adults and children can choose. The activities we present are intended to enhance daily routines and provide sensorimotor strategies for self-regulation (methods to change our levels of alertness through what we see, hear, feel, taste, smell, and how we move). We are confident that you will find within these pages numerous ways to help the child or children you are wanting to support. Many professionals, paraprofessionals, and parents have enjoyed the smiles they've seen as children participate in "taking five."

Overview of the Alert Program
If you are not familiar with the **Alert Program**®, we encourage you to review this brief overview to enhance your use of the *Take Five!* concepts and activities. For additional background information, you

1

may wish to read our book, *"How Does Your Engine Run?"® A Leader's Guide to the Alert Program® for Self-Regulation.* The Leader's Guide describes the steps and activities to support children's ability to attain, maintain, and change their levels of alertness. Children are taught, "If your body is like a car engine, sometimes it runs on high, sometimes it runs on low, and sometimes it runs just right." Through the engine analogy, children learn strategies to change how alert they feel.

There is a state (more accurately, a range) of alertness that can be considered optimal for learning. In this state, children are alert and attentive, they have a "sparkle" in their eye, their muscles are not droopy, and they concentrate with little effort. We want to support children to do all of their learning in this ideal state. For example, when a teacher is introducing a new concept, the children's brains and bodies need to be "just right" for that learning to happen more easily. When parents are teaching children to tie their shoes, the learning will happen most quickly when their nervous systems are in this optimal range.

Through the Alert Program, children learn how to adjust their engine levels. For example, they learn what they can do when their engines are running on "low" before homework time. Likewise, teachers learn what to do when their own engines are running on "low" and the students' engines are running on "high" after lunch recess. Parents learn what to do when their toddlers' engines are still running on "high" two hours past bedtime. Finally, staff and caregivers learn what to do when their clients' engines are on "high" or "low" after a long day at their sheltered workshop.

The Alert Program was initially designed for children with learning and attention difficulties between the ages of 8-12 years. Alert Program concepts, however, have applications for all ages and ability levels because we all need to self-regulate (change how alert we feel). When children are developmentally younger than the age of eight (e.g., those with developmental delays, those with autism or Asperger's Syndrome, and preschoolers), the program can be adapted. When children cannot understand the engine analogy or will not be independent in self-regulation, their parents, teachers, and other school staff will be responsible for developing and offering a repertoire of strategies. Successful adaptations of the Alert Program have been used in a variety of settings. These include homes, regular education classrooms, special education classrooms, inclusion classrooms, camp settings, therapy clinics, and even in settings such as juvenile detention homes, nursing homes, and in traumatic brain injury rehabilitation centers.

2

By learning about self-regulation, all team members (including the parents as the experts on the team) can work together to support children's learning. Even for those who are not utilizing the whole Alert Program, the simple engine vocabulary offers an alternative to the jargon often used by educational teams. Team members have found engine vocabulary useful in describing their observations of children in a non-judgmental manner, serving as a unifying language for the team. For example, by using the engine vocabulary, a parent and teacher might better correspond about Olivia, a preschooler. In the morning, before school, the parent observes that Olivia is having difficulty alerting. The parent could write her observations in a notebook that is passed back and forth from home to school. She might write, "Olivia's engine seems to be in low gear this morning. She might need some extra help to get her engine ready to learn today." The teacher at the end of the school day could write back in the notebook, "You were right. Olivia's engine did need a boost before we started our lessons this morning and some extra help after lunch, but she's leaving now with her engine running 'just right.' Hope you have a good evening." This example also illustrates how the program can be adapted. We would not expect, Olivia, a preschooler, to be independent in self-regulation. She will need her parents and teacher to provide her with options for her engine. The adults in Olivia's life can use the engine vocabulary as a common language to better communicate about her needs.

Even if you do not use the engine vocabulary, we assure you that we have observed many teachers, parents, and therapists significantly improve children's ability to attend and learn by using the *Take Five!* concepts presented in this book. Whether or not children are developmentally old enough to be independent in self-regulation, all students can benefit from having the adults in their lives understand what supports and what compromises the brain's ability to focus, concentrate, learn, remember, and demonstrate knowledge (Oetter & StevensDominguez, 1990).

Special Note

Just to clarify, it is not possible, nor are we recommending, that we attain a "just right" level and stay there all day long. "Just right" is not one specific place or point to strive for. "Just right" is a RANGE in which our brains and bodies function best for different tasks. We can be "just right" for reading quietly in our den but may need to adjust our level of alertness to be "just right" for a football game. Throughout this book, when we describe a "just right state," we could have written instead: "just right range for the task," but this seems too cumbersome.

Why "Take Five?"

Brains need stimulation in order to concentrate and perform well. The old adage, "Sit still and pay attention!" is not physiologically possible. Our bodies can sit still OR pay attention but not both. Think about the "old days" when we used to talk on phones with cords. What did we do when the conversations lasted more than a few minutes? (Remember, the brain cannot sit still and pay attention.) We would twirl the cord in our fingers, doodle on the phone book cover, or pace the few feet back and forth as allowed by the cord. We (supposedly normal adults) need to move in order to pay attention. So what did the phone manufacturers do? They somehow understood this theory and now are making cordless phones!

We want to set up children's nervous systems for success. As mentioned in our *Leader's Guide* and *Introductory Booklet,* the bottom part of the brain (brainstem), the back part of the brain (cerebellum), along with many other parts of the brain are stimulated through heavy work to muscles and joints (activities that involve pushing, pulling, lifting, hanging, climbing, tugging, or towing). When engines are in high gear and participate in heavy work, a message is sent to the rest of the brain and body that says, "Chill out....Calm down....We are not in danger here. We can relax and focus." When engines are in low gear and participate in heavy work, a message is sent to the rest of the brain and body that says, "Be alert! Wake up! We need to get going and focus!"

The beautiful thing about heavy work to muscles and joints is that it helps when engines are in high or low states. There are many ways to "take five." A movement break, including heavy work, is the predominant method that the Alert Program emphasizes to alter one's engine level when it is in "high" or "low" gear. *Take Five!* will expand on this concept by giving examples of ways to help engines by offering heavy work to the whole body (e.g., tug of war), to the hands (e.g., fidgeting with putty), and to the mouth (e.g., chewing gum for heavy work to the jaw joint). This book, also, will explain how to incorporate visual and auditory strategies into learning environments to help children obtain optimal states of alertness.

Five Ways to Change Alert Levels

This *Take Five!* book offers activities to help you to know what to do when "engines are not running just right." In the Alert Program, children (and their adults) learn that when their engines are in a non-optimal state, they can "put something in their mouth, move, touch, look, or listen." These five sensorimotor categories are the main ways to change engine levels. We will use these same categories throughout this book to present the material in an easy-to-follow manner. The categories are somewhat artificial; remember to mix and match the strategies, choosing what works from any and all of the categories.

The title of this book, *Take Five!,* was chosen to highlight the five ways to change engine levels, and at the same time, to remind us to look for ways to take a break and incorporate sensorimotor strategies into our daily routines. We may need a five minute break, a five second break, a fifty minute break, or a five day vacation! Or we may not need a break at all, but need to use strategies to sustain concentration such as chewing gum while reading this book.

Sensory Diets

When teaching the Alert Program to students or when adapting the program for children developmentally younger than the age of eight, the five ways to change engine levels can be considered guidelines to developing a "sensory diet." Occupational therapist, Patricia Wilbarger (1984), coined the term "sensory diet" to describe the brain's need for sensorimotor input (from touch, sight, hearing, taste, smell, or movement), just as our bodies require a nutritional diet. Without input from our senses, our brains experience what could be considered a type of sensory deprivation. If we provide the brain with its needed sensory diet, we will feel alert and attentive. Each person has his or her own unique sensory diet formula with just the right amount and types of sensorimotor activities or environments to stimulate the brain and body. In order to develop a sensory diet for and/or with children, we must be excellent observers of what supports and what compromises optimal functioning. If possible, we suggest that you consult with a local occupational therapist, who uses a sensory integrative approach. She can support you in your observational skills and guide you to the best sensory diet for the student(s) you are working or living with.

Take Five! provides a perspective that supports children and adults to find sensorimotor formulas for success. When choosing activities from this book and considering what daily routines (sensory diets) are best for ourselves and for children, we should be careful to decide what time of day, for how long, and with what intensity we need sensorimotor input (Oetter, 1991). For example, an eight-year-old girl and her mother accidently discovered one element of the daily routine that was crucial. This child had difficulty self-regulating, especially to sleep through the night. After receiving occupational therapy for several months, she was making good progress and sleeping much better. Suddenly one night she was restless and unable to sleep. Together the occupational therapist and the mother brainstormed what changes in the routine might have caused this sudden relapse in her ability to sleep. The mother realized that this particular week her husband was away on a business trip. It wasn't until the child's third restless night that the mother realized the father and daughter's pre-bedtime wrestling routine was far more important to the quality of her sleep than they had understood. Until the father's return, the mother took over the rough-housing with the daughter (providing heavy work to her muscles and joints) and the child returned to her pattern of restful nightly sleep.

Pat Wilbarger (1991-2001; 1995) speaks of the power of an activity. She reminds us to consider that some kinds of sensorimotor input (e.g., heavy work to the whole body, temperature variables, and respiratory activities) have more power to change alert levels than others and that some will last longer than others. In the above example, before bedtime the mother might have tried to help her daughter by giving her a stuffed animal to hold (the touch category), dimming the bedroom lighting (the look category), or playing soft, slow music (the listen category). These all would have been fine choices, but it was the heavy work to her whole body (the move category) that was the most powerful input for changing her alert level and maintaining her ability to sleep through the night.

Understanding Our Own Self-Regulation

We believe that we all must understand what our own adult nervous systems are using for self-regulation to be keen observers of children's self-regulation. If you haven't already, please take a moment now to fill out the *Sensory Motor Preference Checklist (for Adults)* on the following page. (It is also contained in the *Leader's Guide* in a form that can be copied with permission for educational purposes.) This checklist will help you recognize what you are using in your daily routine for your sensory diet.

SENSORY-MOTOR PREFERENCE CHECKLIST (FOR ADULTS)

DIRECTIONS: This checklist was developed to help adults recognize what strategies their own nervous systems employ to attain an appropriate state of alertness. Mark the items below that you use to increase (↑) or to decrease (↓) your state of alertness. You might mark both (↑↓) on some items. Others you might not use at all.

PUT SOMETHING IN YOUR MOUTH (ORAL MOTOR INPUT):

_ drink a milkshake
_ suck on hard candy
_ crunch or suck on ice pieces
_ tongue in cheek movements
_ "chew" on pencil / pen
_ chew on coffee swizzle sticks
_ take slow deep breaths
_ suck, lick, bite on your lips or the inside
  of your cheeks
_ drink carbonated drink
_ eat a cold popsicle
_ eat a pickle

_ chew gum
_ crunch on nuts / pretzels / chips
_ bite on nails / cuticle
_ eat popcorn / cut-up vegetables
_ eat chips and a spicy dip
_ smoke cigarettes
_ chew on buttons, sweatshirt strings or collars
_ whistle while you work
_ drink coffee / tea (caffeinated)
_ drink hot cocoa or warm milk
_ other:

MOVE (VESTIBULAR & PROPRIOCEPTIVE INPUT):

_ rock in a rocking chair
_ shift or "squirm" in a chair
_ push chair back on 2 legs
_ aerobic exercise
_ isometrics / lift weights
_ rock own body slightly
_ scrub kitchen floor
_ roll neck and head slowly

_ sit with crossed legs and bounce one slightly
_ run / jog
_ ride bike
_ tap toe, heel or foot
_ dance
_ tap pencil / pen
_ yard work
_ stretch / shake body parts
_ Other:

TOUCH (TACTILE INPUT):

_ twist own hair
_ move keys or coins in pocket with your hand
_ cool shower
_ warm bath
_ receive a massage
_ pet a dog or cat
_ drum fingers or pencil on table
_ rub gently on skin / clothes

* Fidget with the following:
_ a straw
_ paper clips
_ cuticle / nails
_ pencil / pen
_ earring or necklace
_ phone cord while talking
_ put fingers near mouth, eye, or nose
_ other:

LOOK (VISUAL INPUT):

_ open window shades after a boring movie in a
  classroom
_ watch a fireplace
_ watch fish tank
_ watch sunset / sunrise
_ watch "oil and water" toys

* How do you react to:
_ dim lighting
_ fluorescent lighting
_ sunlight through bedroom window when
  sleeping
_ rose colored room
_ a "cluttered desk" when needing to concentrate

7

LISTEN (AUDITORY INPUT):

_ listen to Classical Music
_ listen to Hard Rock
_ listen to others "hum"
_ work in "quiet" room
_ work in "noisy" room
_ sing or talk to self

* How do you react to:
_ scratch on a chalkboard
_ "squeak" of a mechanical pencil
_ fire siren
_ waking to an unusual noise
_ dog barking (almost constantly)

QUESTIONS TO PONDER

1. Review this Sensory-Motor Preference Checklist. Think about what you do in a small subtle manner to maintain an appropriate alert level that a child with a less mature nervous system may need to do in a larger more intense way.

2. Notice which types of sensory input are comforting to your nervous system and which types of sensory input bother your nervous system. Are your items clustered in a certain category of sensory input?

3. Consider how often (frequency), how long (duration), how much (intensity), and with what rhythm (fast, slow, uneven or even) you use these inputs to change your state of alertness.

4. When you are needing to concentrate at your work space, what sensory input do you prefer to work most efficiently?

   a) What do you put in or around your mouth? (Example: food, drink, gum, etc.)

   b) What do you prefer to touch? (Example: clothing, texture of chair, fidgeting with objects, etc.)

   c) What types of movement do you use? (Example: rock in chair or movement breaks to stretch or walk, etc.)

   d) What are your visual preferences? (Example: natural lighting from window, use of a lamp, brightly colored walls. Are you an "in" person working best with your desk cleared off or an "out" person whose desk is piled high with papers, etc.)

   e) What auditory input do you use? (Example: do you listen to music while you work? If so, what type of beat? Do you like to talk to yourself or others and work at the same time? Do you prefer a quiet environment?, etc.)

Finding What Works For Children

In filling out the *Sensory-Motor Checklist (for Adults)*, we hope you identified the strategies you employ for self-regulation. After we understand what our own adult nervous systems use for self-regulation, we now can consider the child or children you are wanting to support. Notice what children are currently using in each of the five categories and how you can offer more options:

• What do they already put in their mouths? (Do they show a preference for crunchy foods or chewy foods? Do they chew on their pen tops or on the cuff of their shirtsleeves while concentrating?)

• What are they using in the move category? (Do they love to spend time swinging? Do they walk or pace while talking on the phone or telling you a story? Do they like to watch TV, draped upside down over a sofa?)

• What preferences do they show in the touch category? (Do they tap their pencils on the table while thinking? Do they love to snuggle underneath a pile of heavy blankets or with a favorite stuffed animal? What kinds of clothing textures do they prefer to wear?)

• In what type of visual environment do the children work best? (Do they tend to work best when their desk is cleared of all clutter, or do they seem to like to "nest" with lots of paper and things around them while they work? Do they decorate their bedroom with lots of bright colorful wall hangings, or do they prefer few visual distractions in their bedroom?)

• How much and what type of auditory input seems to support the children? (Do they prefer to listen to rock n' roll while they do their homework, or would they rather study in silence? Depending on the task, is there a difference between the children's preference for silence or music in the background? Do they like to listen to music when they are learning new math concepts or only when they are completing their math practice sheets or other familiar seatwork?)

The answers to the above questions are helpful in identifying what the child is using currently for alerting or calming strategies and in determining how to expand his options for self-regulation. Which strategies seem to have the longest effects on his levels of alertness? Which combination of strategies seem to be the right formula to support the child's best functioning? Does he need to make large or subtle shifts in alertness (depending on the demands of the task, the environment, his motivation, or how familiar he is with the task)? When does the child's engine seem to need a change in strategies? How much do they need, with what intensity, at what times of the day?

It is useful to note what time of day the child uses which types of strategies because each individual has their own natural daily cycles (such as their cycle of eating, digesting, or eliminating, cycles of sleep/wake, or cycles of alertness that impact our ability to learn, play, interact, and attend). For many people, after lunch, late afternoon, and early evening can be difficult times to maintain optimal alertness. Watch for what the child is doing at his challenging times of day. What does he seem to crave, or what types of sensorimotor input does he seek? This book is designed to give you many choices for quick and simple activities to provide children with the sensorimotor input they need.

As you begin to choose activities in this book, continue to observe what helps the child to perform at her best. From your observations, you may notice, for example, that she employs few strategies from the mouth category. You must be a good detective and determine if this is due to the student's sensorimotor preference or because chewing gum or biting on pencils is not allowed in the classroom. Our book provides a wide range of activities in each of the sensorimotor categories, so if one type of activity is against the rules, choose another that may be more acceptable in that setting. As you experiment through trial and error, continue to observe what supports the student to focus and attend and what seems to interfere with her ability to function at an optimal level for the task.

One final point: Find what works for your child and develop a daily routine that sets up the nervous system for success. "Play is the work of children. Through play they learn about themselves and the world around them. When all they see, hear, and feel makes sense to them... " we believe their brains and bodies are ready to learn (Sensory Integration International, 1991). Our culture seems to ask us to make a choice between work and play. We suggest instead that our times of work should be enjoyable and that our times of play will be productive.

About the Activities in the Book

This book will describe simple, practical, low-budget ways to support children's learning. In homes and schools, extensive exercise and therapy equipment is not usually available. Most of the *Take Five!*

activities require few materials. A list of resources is provided in the Appendix for purchasing optional items, if budgets permit.

Take Five! is not meant to be a replacement for other needed therapies. There are many difficulties children may experience that necessitate more intervention than what is described in these pages. (See the Caution While Taking Five! section in the Appendix.) Ideally, you are already in contact with an occupational therapist or other professional who can support your child and offer you further understanding of sensory processing theory.

We purposefully selected activities for the book that fit a broad range of cognitive and physical ability levels. These activities can be done individually, in small groups, or in large groups. Not all of the activities will be appropriate for all ages and all types of children. Although some of the examples in the book focus on academic tasks, all activities can be modified for a variety of goals. We are confident that as you read through the activities, you will find many applicable or easily adaptable suggestions for the student(s) you want to support.

The activities included in this book were chosen specifically to help prepare the nervous system for learning. Some activities can be done prior to homework time or between subjects in the classroom. Other activities are meant to support self-regulation while engaged in an academic or other type of task. While all the activities support self-regulation, adults will be pleased to know that these activities also support developmental skills. We hope you will find the activities not only useful, but a "springboard" for your own creative ideas.

To illustrate the need to "take five," let's close by considering homework time. Unfortunately, getting homework completed is often a stressful experience for children (and parents). Many children are giving 110% at school to concentrate and learn. Often they cannot come home after school and give another 110% to complete hours of homework. Sometimes after a long bus or car ride home, children's engines are not ready for focusing on homework. One mother told us her son said after school one day, "Mom, I'm too tired to do my homework. May I go out to rollerblade and then chew some gum?" This child is wise to know that even if his engine is in a low state of alertness, it will be best to "take five" by getting some movement and heavy work to his muscles and joints. He will return in a better state to do his homework. He already knows the point of this book: to find easy ways to "take five" and return to the task refreshed and renewed with engines "running just right!"

Two

Put Something in the Mouth!

PUT SOMETHING IN THE MOUTH!

Patricia Oetter, MA, OTR, FAOTA, is an occupational therapist who discovered the importance of oral motor input while working with one of her "most persistent and patient" teachers: Phillip (Frick, Oetter, & Richter, 1996). From ages three to seven, Phillip showed Patti that activities such as blowing on whistles, playing with bubbles, biting and tugging on soft tubing, sucking on sour lemon drops or crunching on pretzels significantly improved his ability to attend, increased control of his body movements, and supported his air flow for speech. Along with these improvements, Phillip was better able to self-regulate (calm or alert himself) so he could play and interact with his peers. After working with Phillip, Patti continued to refine her theories about the critical role that oral motor input can play in many aspects of therapy. You can learn more about her discoveries in the book, *MORE: Integrating the Mouth with Sensory and Postural Functions* (Oetter, Richter, & Frick, 1995) and in the booklet, *Out of the Mouth of Babes: Discovering the Developmental Significance of the Mouth* (Frick, Frick, Oetter, & Richter, 1996).

We were able to "test drive" some of Patti's oral motor theory along with our engine concepts while working in many classrooms and in a variety of school settings. Over the years, we have had the wonderful opportunity to consult with numerous teachers and other team members. We are firm believers in trying to "lighten the load" for teachers and parents, who already have the full-time jobs of educating and raising children. In our consultations, we try to assist school staff and parents to meet the difficult demands of their often overloaded schedules and at the same time support self-regulation. We developed these *Take Five!* activities in the schools, simultaneously meeting teachers' and parents' goals while helping children remain alert for learning. In this chapter we will share with you the oral motor activities that teachers and parents have reported to be successful.

As we help children to "take five," we must be aware of all the mouth strategies they already are using to help them to concentrate and focus. For example, children will often put things in their mouths while they are listening to an adult read a story aloud. They may chew on sweatshirt strings, collars, cuffs, pencils, erasers, or their hair (if it's long enough). Even as adults, we continue to use oral motor input to help us to stay attentive while engaged in tasks; when we are sitting in a long meeting, some of us chew on jewelry, the inside of the mouth, fingernails, cuticles, or pen tops. Also, what foods we choose to eat can be influenced by their calming or alerting qualities. For example, think what you like to eat for

13

breakfast: do you like soft, warm oatmeal; chewy, hot bagels; tart, juicy grapefruit; or cold, crunchy granola? In addition to chewing and biting, we know from stress reduction techniques that slow, deep breaths can calm us and when we are feeling stressed, we breathe in a more quick and shallow manner.

We can self-regulate with our mouths using food and non-food items. First, we'll discuss the food items, but if you are thinking of a child for whom weight, allergies, or sugar sensitivities are a concern, just know that we'll be covering non-food activities as well. Remember to choose from these examples whatever supports the child. Avoid those that interfere with his best functioning.

Food Items

We've all had the experience of eating when we weren't hungry. This can be a sign that our body is wanting a certain kind of sensory input for self-regulation reasons. (We won't go into all the reasons we may crave certain types of foods, but for the purpose of this book, just consider that one reason could be that we choose certain foods to help us to be calm or alert.) When you are watching a long movie, do you enjoy eating crunchy popcorn, chewing Sour Patch Kids, or drinking an ice cold lemonade?

In general, foods that are alerting tend to be cold, sour/tart, spicy, minty, or crunchy. Foods that are calming tend to be warm, smooth, or sweet. Some foods fall under the heavy work category, giving heavy work to the jaw and cheek muscles; therefore **they can help to either alert or calm.** Note that there is a wide range of individual differences in the alerting and calming qualities of food, so use these as general guidelines and as you try options, be sure to observe what best supports children's performance.

The following list gives examples of types of foods you can consider offering your student for self-regulation. Experiment and try unusual combinations. Sometimes we must go beyond our own preferences and comfort zone to offer foods that we ordinarily would not select. You might be surprised (as we were initially) to find preschoolers who like beef jerky or chips with red hot salsa to jump start their engines in the morning! (Of course, parents know their children best and will want to advise other team members whether certain foods or activities should be avoided because of food allergies, dietary restrictions, difficulties with chewing, sucking, and swallowing, latex sensitivities, or for any other reasons).

Food Items To Help Engines

Parents can experiment at home and determine which foods, at which time of the day, with what intensity support children to function throughout the day. Through trial and error, parents will discover which foods are best to serve for breakfast, to pack in a lunchbox, or to offer after school. They may find that providing a plate of frozen grapes to suck or chew, crunchy pretzels to dip into spicy mustard, and a cold, partially frozen cranberry juice drink to sip through a straw might be the perfect snack to complement homework time.

Long car rides can be another challenge for self-regulation. Parents can guide children to gather oral motor items for a "travel pack." If their engines tend to go into "low" gear in the car, choose items that are alerting. If their engines tend to go in to "high" gear, choose items that are calming. When in doubt, choose items that provide "heavy work." Whenever possible, encourage children to participate in the decision- making process and assist in loading their favorite foods into their "travel pack." Read on for non-food items to add to the "travel pack," along with suggestions from the other four categories of ways to "take five."

Kindergarten teachers quite easily incorporate the use of oral motor strategies in their daily routines. Usually, children in kindergarten have snack time. We might want to expand on the variety of foods to support self-regulation in children who need intensity to change their engine speeds by offering crunchy foods, sour foods, chewy foods, spicy foods, tart juice drinks, or food and non-food items to suck on (see above list for examples). Also, the timing of snacks can be important when trying to help children stay in an optimal state for learning. For example, snack time can prepare the brain and body to focus, so it's ideal to schedule circle time right after snack time.

Note: Children who do not have good control of the muscles in their mouth can tug, bite, and pull on a washcloth soaked in tart juice and then frozen. Others have found placing items to chew inside cheesecloth and then helping to place it in the mouth prevents unwanted swallowing of gum or choking for children with poor oral motor control.

Examples Of Foods That Are . . .

SWEET: sweet rolls, raisins, candies, applesauce, or sweet potatoes

CHEWY: string cheese or cheese cut into cubes, bagels, dried fruit, gum (perhaps more than one piece to provide the intensity needed), fruit roll-ups, raisins, Starburst, Gummy Bears, or other chewy candy

CRUNCHY: pretzels, nuts, raw vegetables, popcorn, apples, chips, granola, raw pasta, rice cakes, or necklace of Cheerios

SOUR/TART: cranberries, grapefruit, tart lemonade, pickles, lemon or lime wedges, Tear Jerkers, War Heads, or other sour candies

SPICY: hot salsa, Red Hots or Hot Tamale candies, red cinnamon jellybeans, or cinnamon gum

COLD: popsicles, snow cones, frozen grapes, frozen bananas, frozen peas or diced carrots, frozen licorice, ice cold drink, or flavored ice cubes crushed into ice chips

WARM: hot chocolate, warm soup, mashed potatoes, oatmeal, baked potatoes, buttered toast, or hot tea

SUCKING: hard candy, citrus fruit wedges, lollipops, a candy (or real) pacifier, or using a straw to suck up applesauce, pudding, yogurt, or Jello (for intensity)

BLOWING: in bubble gum or with a straw into milk (We mention these two options because they are common ways children enjoy exploring orally. Usually, adults prefer blowing activities that do not involve food. See blowing activities in this chapter).

TUGGING/BITING/PULLING: on licorice, beef jerky, fruit leather, taffy, Sugar Daddy or Bit O' Honey candy, a straw, or soft, rubber tubing

Brain Food

In upper grade levels, we have observed many creative teachers who support children's learning through oral motor strategies. In some classrooms, teachers offer food to support engines, but they refer to the food as "brain food" (Oetter, 1983) to distinguish it from foods eaten to satisfy hunger. After explaining why the students will use the "brain food" and after setting up rules around its use, the teacher chooses how to offer the oral motor strategies. Some teachers have a container filled with hard candy, fruit roll-ups, or pretzels on their desk where students "power up" their engines any time throughout the day. Other teachers pass out the "brain food" to the whole class to "take five" or for only a particular task. For example, before the teacher reads a book aloud to her students, she may pass out paper cups of popcorn to help their engines stay alert for listening to the story. Writing a note home to parents, explaining the use of the oral motor input, and asking parents to send snacks for children to keep in their desks or backpacks is a low-budget option.

Non-Food Items

There are numerous non-food options for self-regulation involving the mouth. We will cover a few here, and specific activity examples will follow. Depending on the task, the environment, and the "rules," it is useful to consider both food and non-food items for children. For example, in some classrooms chewing gum is forbidden. In these classrooms, we suggest using straws to chew on (the kind of straw with the flexible neck is best). This is an especially easy strategy to use at home or school, providing good chewing input (heavy work to the jaw) without food intake. Typically, the reason for the "no gum rule" is that administrators are worried that gum will end up in carpets, stuck under chairs, or even in children's hair. Straws come with few complications. They are inexpensive, readily available, and do not stick to anything. You don't even have to worry about cleaning them; just throw them away when students are finished.

Don't get us wrong. While straws are a good substitute, we believe children should be allowed to use gum for self-regulation. Some children need several pieces of gum in their mouth at the same time to support their need for intensity and heavy work to their jaw. Numerous teachers have found that if rules are clearly stated and enforced, children easily can learn the proper use (and disposal) of gum.

Exercise Water Bottles

Exercise water bottles provide another simple oral motor strategy. Many classroom teachers have each of their students keep an exercise

16

water bottle on their desk. For some students, sipping or sucking on their water bottle as they work keeps their engines running just right. Others may use it only when they are thirsty or not at all. Water bottles are also useful at home during homework time and in the car on long drives. When budgets are limited, teachers can ask parents to supply water bottles. There are many variations of bottles and canteens with different types of tops and diameters of straws, all requiring different kinds of mouth closure and strength for sucking. Children can choose which is best for them based on their preferences. Another low-cost option is to ask a local restaurant to donate "to go" cups with lids and straws for classroom use.

Sucking and Blowing Activities

In general, sucking and blowing through straws hold unlimited possibilities for self-regulation strategies. (More to come when you read the activities in this chapter.) Occupational therapists often emphasize lots of blowing and sucking activities and we don't even get commission on straw sales! We recommend these activities because the same trunk and chest muscles that support breath, support posture needed to sit upright at a desk. Also, deep breathing supports self-regulation and helps engines to be in an optimal state for learning. In addition, when blowing or sucking involves an element of watching (e.g., blowing a cottonball with a straw) the eye muscles are set up to focus and work together for reading and writing. The book, *MORE: Integrating The Mouth With Postural And Sensory Functions,* (Oetter, Richter, & Frick, 1995) explains in more detail the importance of breath support and its connection to oral motor and vision function.

Now for a brief physics lesson about straws and the possibilities for intensity. The longer the straw, the more work it takes to suck the liquid. Likewise, the smaller the diameter of the straw, the more work it takes to suck the liquid. The thicker the liquid, the more work it takes to suck the liquid. (Ah ha, we see the theme of heavy work to the mouth as the emphasis here!). Whether using food or non-food items, help children to experiment with the length, diameter, and type of straws used. Also, children can experiment with the consistency of what they suck through the straw, such as milkshakes, yogurt shakes, fruit smoothies, applesauce, pudding, jello, or semi-frozen fruit juice "slushes." Non-food substances can be used, such as blowing through a straw into soft putty to make one large bubble. **This putty can be made by combining two parts Elmer's white glue (not water based school glue) with one part liquid starch.**

17

Tubing

Soft, rubber tubing is another versatile oral motor strategy. Occupational therapists often can supply parents and teachers with Theratubing, a soft tubing made with latex rubber (non-latex tubing is also available). If you want to buy your own, refer to the Appendix for a list of suppliers. Theratubing comes in different colors, diameters, and amounts of resistance for biting or pulling. Inexpensive options for tubing include oxygen tubing available from hospital supply companies or freezer tubing (used in refrigerator ice makers) from hardware stores. Tubing can be soaked in vanilla to remove the noxious taste: place a length of tubing in a bowl, just barely cover the tubing with water, add 1 teaspoon of vanilla extract, and soak over night. Cleaning tubing in a dishwasher is not recommended. It can be cleaned with one part chlorine bleach to ten parts water, or use a dental disinfecting solution. (See Appendix for a list of resources.)

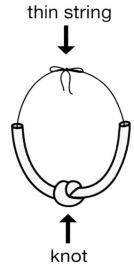

thin string

knot

For young children, a tubing necklace can be created by cutting a length of tubing and tying a knot. Be sure that the necklace is long enough to avoid the hazard of choking and provide supervision. Or for safety, thread a very thin piece of string through a short length of tubing and tie a knot at the center of the tubing. (See illustration.) In this way, under tension, the necklace will break. Another option is to attach the tubing to a pacifier clip available at most department stores. For older children, a 2" length of tubing can be placed over the eraser of a pencil or pen top. Watch that the children do not bite off a small piece of the tubing and swallow it. Put your detective hat on: If a child is biting off pieces of the tubing, was the tubing providing enough intensity? No. So you might want to try a partially frozen piece of licorice instead of the tubing to provide more intensity and avoid any danger to the child.

Music

Musical instruments that involve blowing are another fine oral motor strategy for home or school use. For inexpensive options, we recommend kazoos or harmonicas. Waxed paper over combs are good too, but they require a bit more coordination. When guiding children to other musical instruments for band or music lessons, you might want to share with them how blowing can help engines to self-regulate. The blowing required for woodwinds and brass instruments may prove to be helpful for self-regulation and very organizing to the nervous system. It's curious to us which children choose to play the tuba and which choose the piccolo (a big difference in intensity for blowing, coordination, and heavy work for carrying the instrument). We are emphasizing instruments that involve blowing in this

chapter, but drums could be an excellent choice for children who prefer strategies in the move or touch categories to help their engines. Again, the timing of when children use the strategy is important. For example, a father might suggest that his daughter "take five" and practice her trombone in the middle of homework time. The father could draw a stop sign on the math sheet. After completing 15 math problems, the child sees the stop sign. She is reminded it would be a good time to take a short break and practice the trombone. The child should come back refreshed and ready to complete her math homework more easily.

Other music activities can be excellent ways to "take five." We can "whistle while we work" and at the same time prepare our nervous systems to be attentive to the task. Teachers can ask children to hum or whistle a familiar song while they are clearing off their desks to prepare for a spelling test. At the end of the song, hopefully children's engines will be in an optimal state for demonstrating their knowledge on the test. Another way teachers use music strategies with the whole class is to "take five" between subjects by encouraging everyone to sing a song together. Adding movement such as marching to the music helps engines all the more. Singing instructions to children is another good way to use breath for self-regulation and to add novelty for better listening. Ask children to sing the instructions back, so they get the benefit of deep exhales, too.

Parents can use these same oral motor and respiratory activities at home. Homework time may proceed more smoothly when rhythm and singing are involved. Young children can play with making funny sounds to encourage deep breathing for self-regulation such as barking, howling, hissing, or babbling sounds like "bbbbb," "eeeee," "mmmmm." Older children enjoy trying to say tongue twisters or making "fish faces."

Remember to look for what enhances self-regulation. Trying a variety of strategies and activities makes it more likely that you will find the combinations of oral motor input that works to support engines. The following activities are more examples of oral motor games for self-regulation that we have used in numerous classrooms and homes. Teachers, parents, and therapists give their stamp of approval. We're sure the children will enjoy them, too!

19

Bundle of Straws

Materials:
3 drinking straws per person
1 rubberband per person
bubble solution or dishwashing liquid

Here's How:
1. Cut the 3 drinking straws in half. This gives you 6 mini-straws.
2. Put the rubberband around the 6 mini-straws to bundle them together.
3. Dip one end of the bundle into the bubble solution, remove.
4. Then blow through the non-dipped end to provide a beautiful cascade of bubbles!

Things We Noticed:
- As with all bubble blowing activities, a quick review of the difference between blowing and sucking may be important for some children. For children who accidently might suck when they need to blow, you might want to try blowing bubbles in water, milk, or juice to avoid bubble solution in the mouth.

- This is a great activity for children of many different ability levels. Some children are not able to close their lips tightly around a single straw, but they will most likely be able to blow enough air through at least one of the six straws in the bundle to be successful in producing at least one bubble. Those with more sophisticated cheek and lip muscle coordination, along with good air flow, can easily earn the title of "Bubble Machine!"

- To make this activity more challenging, one child can try to blow bubbles for a long period of time while another child or adult counts, "one Mississippi, two Mississippi . . . "

- Another variation is to have one child blow bubbles while another attempts to pop the bubbles with a finger, counting each pop out loud. This is a way to reinforce counting and one-to-one correspondence for early childhood education.

20

Bubble Pipe

Materials:

1 styrofoam cup per person
1 drinking straw per person
bubble solution or dishwashing liquid

Here's How:

1. Push the tip of the drinking straw through the side of the cup. Aim for the lower quarter of the side of the cup. No glue, no tape, no mess! Nothing is needed to keep the straw in the side of the cup.

2. Pour a little bubble solution into the cup so that the level of solution is just above the straw.

3. Blow air through the straw and watch the bubbles rise up in the cup, creating your very own bubble pipe.

Things We Noticed:

• This activity is best for those children who can understand the basic physics concept of keeping the cup lower than the level of their mouth and the straw tilted downward from their mouth.

• Children enjoy this activity the most when they can close their lips tightly around a single straw and when they have enough hand control to not tip the cup.

• As with many of the blowing activities, the bubble pipe can be fun to take in the bath tub or play with at the kitchen sink. At school, teachers often use sand or water play tables for blowing activities or go outside to play with the bubbles.

21

Mountain of Bubbles _____

Materials:

1-2 straws or 12″ length of Theratubing per person (see the Appendix)
dish pan
water
dishwashing liquid
rubber or plastic puzzle pieces and formboard (or laminated 3″ x 5″ cards)
paper towels
Optional: No More Tears Shampoo or 3″ x 5″ cards (laminated)

Here's How:

1. Place a squirt of dishwashing liquid or No More Tears Shampoo into the dishpan.

2. Put about 1/2″ of water into the dishpan.

3. Place the puzzle pieces into the pan with the soapy water.

4. Place the puzzle formboard beside the pan on paper towels.

5. Here's the fun part . . . blow through the straw, making sure that the bottom of the straw is in the soap solution. If done correctly, as you continue to blow, this will result in lots of bubbles, hence the name: Mountain of Bubbles!

6. Once your mountain is nice and high, stop blowing. Use a finger to pop the bubbles so that the soapy water and the puzzles pieces become visible.

7. Pick one puzzle piece out of the solution, dry it off, and place it into the formboard.

8. Start over again at step #5 . . . Continue to blow in the soapy water, make a mountain of bubbles, pop the bubbles, pick out a puzzle piece, and then place it into the formboard until the puzzle is complete.

Things We Noticed:

• The reason you might want to choose a tear-free shampoo is that the mountain of bubbles looks so appealing that many young children cannot resist putting their whole face into it.

• This activity is so easy to adapt for all different ages and learning levels that you should feel free to go wild with dreaming up your own personal adaptations. To get you started, here are a few we've tried:

a) Matching Game: Instead of puzzle pieces, use 3″ x 5″ cards to make your own game that will be particularly interesting for the children's learning level. Make your own set of 3″ x 5″ cards by drawing colors, shapes, or numbers on them. Then laminate them. In the schools we laminate everything, but if you are a parent and access to a laminating machine is more difficult, try your local copy store. Place one set of cards beside the dishpan and place the other set of cards into the soapy water. Do the activity in the same manner as described in the Mountain of Bubble activity. Each time you blow the bubbles and pop them, reach into the water, grab a card, and match it to the dry set. Repeat until all cards are matched.

b) Questions Game: By using 3″ x 5″ cards, this activity has endless possibilities because you can write anything on the card for any academic level. Simply write any type of question on the 3″ x 5″ cards and laminate them. Then continue as you did above: blow the bubbles, pop the bubbles, reach into the water, pick a card, and answer the question. Children can practice their math facts, their reading or spelling words and have so much fun they probably won't even know they are working!

c) When the goal is to help children work on speech and language development, place objects (rather than puzzle pieces or 3″ x 5″ cards) into the dishpan for the child to name. For example, when trying to support the child to make the initial "f" sound in words, objects in the dishpan would all begin with the letter "f", such as a plastic frog, flag, foot, etc. The child blows bubbles, pops the bubbles, picks one object from the soapy water, names it, and then repeats by blowing more bubbles, etc.

d) When two people blow bubbles, one on either side of the dishpan, children can improve in communication skills. For example, an adult and child can both blow in the dishpan. It is natural for eyes to meet, even mouths to turn upright in smiles, and turns to be taken in blowing . . . all precursors to verbal turn-taking for conversations.

NOTE: This activity was first observed at Albuquerque Therapy Services.

Roads with Cottonballs

Materials:
1 straw per person
1 package of cottonballs
a piece of butcher paper
1 black marker
Optional: magazines

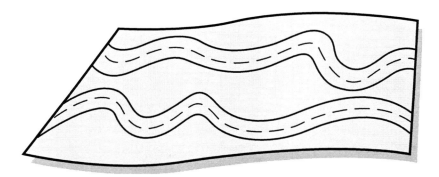

Here's How:
1. Draw a road(s) on the butcher paper with a marker (see illustration). Our students enjoyed the deluxe version where we collected magazine pictures of trucks and 4-wheel drive vehicles to glue onto the butcher paper.

2. Laminate the butcher paper, if possible.

3. Participants each have their own straw. Each child blows one cottonball across the paper, "driving" carefully to stay on the road. It really isn't a race. We encourage practicing to attain future driver's licenses. In this way, staying on the road is the focus.

Things We've Noticed:
- If you don't have cottonballs handy, you can tear off a piece of paper and crumple it to make a paper wad for blowing. Raiding the recycle bin is a good source of paper for this activity.

- We typically used this game as a way to set up the eyes and engines to focus before other academic tasks. It can be a "take five" break between subjects or for a break in homework time.

- A silly variation: Place a trash can at the end of a table. Children blow the cottonball across the table into the trash can. You can place the butcher paper road on top of the table, but even without the paper road, we were surprised to see how much joy children received from such a simple variation.

24

Sheep Herding Game

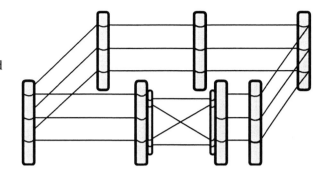

Materials:
1 straw per person
1 package of cottonballs
1 piece of butcher paper or large posterboard
1 dark colored marker

Here's How:
1. Draw a picture of a sheep pen on the paper. Don't panic. Those who consider themselves to be artistically challenged can just draw a big version of this shape:

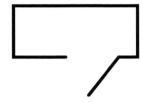

2. Scatter cottonballs on the paper, outside the pen. You may notice that the cottonballs look suspiciously like sheep.

3. Use the straw to blow the cottonballs, one at a time, through the open gate, and into the pen. Another option is to draw a pen that is closed, a big version of this shape:

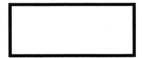

Then the child can make the sheep jump over the fence by sucking air up through the straw to lift the cottonball off the paper and moving it into the pen.

Things We Noticed:
• This activity can be used to practice basic math concepts:

Addition example: An adult can ask a child, "What is 3 + 4?" The child would blow 3 sheep into the pen, then 4 sheep, and count the number of sheep to find the answer.

Subtraction example: In the same manner, starting with 7 sheep in the pen, one could ask, "What is 7-3?" The child would take 3 sheep out of the pen, and then count how many sheep are left to find the answer.

25

- While playing the Sheep Herding Game, two children can practice their math facts together in the classroom or at home. The first child who has the list of math problems could ask the second child the math problem. The sheep would be moved and the first child would record the answer on the math sheet. After a certain number of problems were completed, they could reverse roles.

- For long term use, we find that it is best to laminate or cover the paper with plastic. When young children are concentrating, they can drool. This isn't a serious problem unless you would like to preserve the sheep pen for future use.

- We developed this game while working with Navajo children who were quite familiar with sheep herding. We suggest adapting the activity to create a game that would be of interest to the children in your area. Just a reminder: These activities are helping to set up the nervous system to be ready to learn. You might want to do them before an academic task or as a "take five" break from the academic task to help engines keep running just right.

Here are a few variations we've heard of:

a) Draw a design that looks like the roads in a town on the paper. Have children blow the cottonball, as though it was a car, to different stores or addresses, etc.

b) Draw a soccer field, football field, or an ice hockey rink on the paper. Use the cottonball as a soccer ball, football, or puck moving it by blowing through the straw.

Blowing to the Number Game _____

Materials:

1 straw per person

math problems on a worksheet or math flash cards

ten cards (ten 5" x 8" cards or five 8 1/2" x 11" pieces of paper cut in
    half to yield 10 cards)

Here's How:

1. Write the numbers 0-9, one number per card.

2. In front of the child, place the cards numbered 0-9 on the floor or
    on a tabletop in a semi-circle.

3. Someone reads the math problem or shows the child a math flash
    card. The child uses the straw to blow the cottonball to the card,
    indicating the correct answer to the problem. The answer is re-
    corded. Repeat the process to complete all the problems.

Things We've Noticed:

- This is a great activity to help children practice math concepts
    without requiring more paper and pencil time. It's perfect for
    homework time or as a learning center in a classroom.

- Rather than blowing the cottonball to the correct answer, children
    can throw a Koosh ball to the card, indicating the answer. This
    would be a "take five" activity using touch as the means to support
    self-regulation rather than blowing.   Some children like to challenge
    their balance by sitting on a T-stool (see Appendix) or milking
    stool while tossing the Koosh ball to the cards.

- For preschoolers or other developmentally younger children, the
    cards could have colors, shapes, or letters drawn on them. Children
    could blow the cottonball in the above manner to practice their
    pre-academic skills.

"No Hands" Math

Materials:
1 straw per person
1 pack of math flash cards (or make your own set of personalized math problems on 3" x 5" cards)
1 package of cottonballs

Here's How:
1. Child picks one card and reads the math problem.

2. By sucking air up through the straw, the child moves the correct number of cottonballs, one at a time, onto the card. This is a "no hands" lifting approach.

3. Child picks another card, lays it down on the table, and answers the problem in the same manner.

4. When all the math flash cards are completed, the child can record his answer on a math sheet or ask an adult or older child to check his work.

Things We've Noticed:
• This activity is excellent for homework time or as a learning center in the classroom.

• For preschoolers or developmentally younger children, rather than math flash cards, they could practice one-to-one correspondence. Place stickers on cards, each card with a different number of stickers. For example, one card could have one rabbit sticker on it, another card could have two rabbit stickers on it, etc. By sucking air up through the straw, the child moves the correct number of cottonballs, one on each sticker (adding a fluffy white tail to each rabbit). Other color or letter matching activities can be created, too. Use your imagination!

28

Mosaic Art Project _____

Materials:
1 straw per person
one 8 1/2" x 11" colored construction paper per person
Elmer's glue or glue stick
1/2" pieces of differently colored construction paper (children can
   help to tear the paper)

Here's How:
1. Lay 1/2" pieces of paper on a table next to the 8 1/2" x 11" paper.

2. Spread glue on the 8 1/2" x 11" paper in a large area (soon to be
   filled with the small pieces of paper).

3. By sucking up air through the straw, move one small piece of
   paper onto the glued area.

4. Continue to complete the design.

Things We've Noticed:
- This activity can be adapted for preschoolers and others at a pre-
  academic level. For example, to practice matching colors, draw a
  rainbow on a piece of paper. Then have the children move all the
  small, yellow pieces onto the yellow section of the rainbow, etc.

- On holidays, children can move the small pieces of paper by sucking up air through the straw to "color in" a picture that corre-
  sponds to the holiday. For example on St. Patrick's Day, children
  can move green pieces of paper onto a picture of a shamrock.

29

Party Blowers

Materials:

1 party blower per person (available in the party section of
   department stores)
3" x 5" cards
Optional: Fischer Price Toy People

Here's How:

1. The child will need some time to just play with the blower. This, in and of itself, can be a "take five" break or preparation for other academic tasks.

2. Fold the 3" x 5" card in half so that it forms a "v" shape.

3. Write the applicable academic problems (e.g., math facts, reading words, shapes, or colors) on the 3" x 5" cards.

4. Place the "v" card on a table so the card can stand by itself (looks like an upside down "v."

5. Line up several cards on the table.

6. Blow into the party blower so that a card moves across the table or is knocked over.

7. Solve the problem on that card.

8. Take another turn in the same manner.

Things We've Noticed:

• This activity has limitless possibilities. Go wild! Have fun! Make your own games.

• When you make up your own games, they could include matching concepts (color, shape, size), identification concepts (letters, numbers, words), or directionality concepts (on, over, under, beside).

• For preschoolers, on a table or floor set up Fischer Price Toy People or other knock-downable toys. Blow the party blowers, knocking down the toys.

• We've found that party blowers have a limited life span. They do break and fall apart easily. Luckily, they are inexpensive.

30

Comments:

- Most occupational therapists get very jazzed about the therapeutic use of whistles (as well they should). As mentioned earlier, blowing supports self-regulation and helps the eyes to focus. It's a perfect activity to do before reading or other activities where the eyes will need to work together.

- The book, *MORE: Integrating the Mouth with Sensory and Postural Functions* (Oetter, Richter, & Frick, 1995), goes into great depth about all the wonderful benefits of using whistles, as well as categorizing and grading whistles according to their therapeutic value. You may want to consult your local occupational therapist who is trained in sensory integration regarding the best choice of whistles for the children you have in mind.

- Cleaning whistles: You can clean whistles in a solution of one part chlorine bleach to 10 parts water or buy a dental disinfecting solution (see Appendix) that is a bit gentler on whistle parts.

- Blowing whistles in a classroom or family group is quite fun. You can purchase harmonicas, kazoos, and siren whistles quite inexpensively (see Appendix). All can blow on their whistles and experiment with their breath. See how long you can sustain the sound. Try to make low, deep sounds or try to imitate a sequence of different variations (e.g., quick, quick, slow, slow). Children enjoy having conversations with the whistles taking turns "talking" with one another. By varying the pitch, length, and sound of the whistle you can imitate sentences, questions, or exclamations. Pretend it is an understandable conversation. Be dramatic and listen for the giggles!

- Most whistles make noise and this can be really helpful or really distressing to different people, depending how the sound affects their engines. The following activity describes the use of the rainbow corncob pipe. In our experience, this quiet whistle can be incorporated easily into homes and classrooms. Children are delighted to blow them and watch the rainbow colored string as they blow.

Rainbow Corncob Pipe

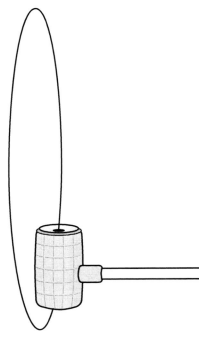

Materials:
1 rainbow corncob pipe (See Appendix)

Here's How:
1. Assemble the rainbow corncob pipe by placing the white, plastic straw into the corncob.

2. At first, as the child learns to blow the pipe, it is easiest if the string is held up high, vertical to the ground. Then instruct the child to blow while releasing the string.

3. Play with all the possibilities of ways to twist and turn the pipe to make the rainbow string move.

4. The adults might be interested in watching the children's eyes as they blow the pipe.

What We've Noticed:
• This is a great activity to do before paper/pencil or reading tasks because it not only helps with levels of alertness, it gets our eyes set up to focus and work well together.

• The rainbow corncob pipes don't make noise while blowing. These are not the only whistles that can be beneficial, but they are quiet, making it easier to incorporate them into classrooms. Children and adults, alike, love them.

• If a child has difficultly blowing the rainbow corncob pipe, it may be that she has poor coordination of her lips, eyes, or breath support. Consult an occupational therapist in your area for suggestions.

• To clean a rainbow corncob pipe, you can place the white, plastic straw into a dishwasher. Or you can clean in the same manner as mentioned in the previous page.

Three

Move!

MOVE!

Movement breaks may be one of the most common ways to "take five." This comes naturally for many of us. If you are seated for an extended period of time, you might roll your neck, stand up to stretch, or take a walk, even just down the hall at work. You come back to your desk, re-energized and ready to concentrate again. These are the simple types of brief movement breaks we will be suggesting in this chapter.

In order to help us remain alert, our bodies crave different types of movement, with varying degrees of intensity, for differing amounts of time, and at different times of the day (Oetter, 1991). This is true in all the categories (mouth, move, touch, look, and listen), but it is the most obvious to illustrate in the move category.

For example, you might be a person who enjoys jogging three miles each morning before work (an intense form of movement for a pro-longed period of time). To run after work would seem unnatural to you, perhaps even useless since your body needs a jump start to be ready for the day. And for someone else to run after work or before bed would be the perfect "cool down" for the day. Another person might take a brisk walk around the neighborhood after work (of moderate intensity and amount of time), but to walk before work would not feel natural. Yet another person may find that to take a brief, slow, stroll through the park (a less intense form of movement and of shorter length) at lunch time is the perfect type of movement to stay alert for the afternoon. And then there are those of us who know we should exercise, know it would feel good to our bodies, but just don't quite find the time or the energy to get the ideal type of movement each day. If this sounds like you, don't be distressed; as you continue to work on your New Year's resolution to get more exercise, you probably are using strategies from the other catego-ries to maintain an alert state such as crunching on carrots (mouth), fidgeting with paperclips at your desk (touch), keeping the window shades wide open (look), or listening to music in the background while you work (listen).

Variations of Intensity

Adults crave different types of movement with different degrees of intensity than children do. In normal development, children move in ways that are bigger, stronger, longer, louder, and harder than our own. What do we, the adults, do? We call it a "behavior problem!"

James, an active seven-year-old boy, craves lots of movement in order to attend. He cannot sit still and pay attention. While his teacher reads a story aloud to the class, she enjoys rocking in her

33

rocking chair. James tries his hardest to follow the rules, but inevitably, usually without even knowing it, he starts to rock on the back two legs of his chair. Now, if the principal walked by the classroom at this point, she might think James is misbehaving and the teacher sitting in her rocker is acting appropriately. In fact, James is doing exactly what his body needs to do to attend to the story. And if we asked James, he probably could repeat the whole story in detail. If the teacher is concerned that James may fall out of his chair, she might suggest placing a small, slightly inflated, beach ball on top of his seat, so he can get the back and forth movement his body is craving to help him to attend. (See activity page for an explanation of the use of beach balls and other seating options.)

As you begin helping children to find ways to "take five" in the move category, keep in mind that you want to help them to find the kind of movement they need with the right intensity, for an adequate amount of time and at the correct time of day (or number of times in the day). One parent discovered that if he wanted to have a "heart to heart" talk with his son, it was best to do it after school, while they were both stacking firewood. This type of heavy work with great intensity for about 30 minutes after school was the right formula for the father and son to communicate well with each other.

Ways to Move

In the *Leader's Guide* (pg. 2-9), we address the six different ways to move. The words we use with children to describe these movements are: "heavy work, up and down, front and back, upside down, crash and bump, and circles." Examples of movement breaks are organized according to these six different ways in the following pages.

All of us, typically, use some strategies from each of the six different ways to move to adjust our engine levels as needed throughout the day. **In general, slow, rhythmical movement can be calming, and fast, arrhythmical movement can be alerting.** For example, if James' teacher sits on her rocking chair, moving back and forth in a slow, rhythmical manner, it will be calming to her nervous system. If another person sits on the rocking chair and quickly moves back and forth in a jerky fashion, it will be alerting to the nervous system. **When in doubt, do heavy work because it is effective when engines are in low or high states of alertness.** We have included activities in all six ways of moving, but we recommend beginning with the heavy work options.

At School

In classrooms, we have observed teachers incorporating movement strategies into their daily routines in a variety of ways. Teachers can support students' self-regulation needs individually or as a whole group. A teacher might observe one student's engine going into high while he is doing his seatwork. She might suggest in a positive tone of voice, "Terrell, it looks to me like your engine is not in the best place for learning right now. Perhaps it would be easier to get your work done if you 'take five.' Would you please carry this box of paper down to the office for me? I bet you'll come back with your engine running just right!" Between subjects, a teacher might tell her whole class, "Let's get our minds and bodies ready for our new science lesson. Let's stand up and sing the Head, Shoulders, Knees and Toes song as fast as we can to wake up our bodies. Then we'll all be ready to begin our science lesson."

At Home

At home, parents can help children determine how much, for how long, and at what time of the day movement is needed for their sensory diets. Just as we mentioned in our earlier example about adults choosing different types of movement (jogging, brisk walking, or strolling), children will engage in a wide variety of movement activities to self-regulate. Some children, in order to get their engines up and running, need heavy work first thing in the morning. For example, when the parent goes into the bedroom to awaken the child, the parent and child might play tug-of-war with the blankets before going to eat breakfast. Other children need to get movement right after school and before they start their homework. Parents might suggest that children go outside to ride their bikes around the neighborhood or play on the backyard swings. Many other activities are included in this chapter from which parents and children can choose the most appropriate.

Just a reminder about the timing of the movement: when choosing activities, remember that movement will prepare the body to be ready to focus and concentrate. If children help out with chores in the family, it might be best to do them right before homework time. For example, carrying a laundry basket filled with clothes from the basement, upstairs to the bedrooms, could be a way to "take five" before sitting down to do homework. Or for children who have difficulty sitting to eat dinner with the family, vacuuming the living room carpet beforehand may prepare the child's engine to run "just right" for conversing and eating at the dinner table. Also, using strategies during dinner can help adjust or maintain engine levels.

End Products
One last thought about organizing movement activities for

self-regulation. When children are moving, they can escalate (or overload), getting louder and louder and moving faster and faster. Their nervous systems get disorganized. When children are engaged in focused heavy work activities this is less likely to happen since children will rarely escalate when there is an "end product." An end product is a task requiring a moment of concentration. For example, imagine children following an obstacle course in the home, crawling over and under furniture. This would be an excellent movement activity, but children could rev up their engines so high that they would not be in an optimal state to return to school work, or homework after the activity.

By placing a task at the end of the obstacle course, children would have a moment to stop, focus, complete the task, and then get up and move again. The task could be placing a puzzle piece into a formboard each time they complete the obstacle course. Or the task could be writing the answer to one math problem on a homework sheet each time they complete the obstacle course. **When using end products in this manner, children have periods of movement followed by periods of concentration. This is an ideal formula to maintain optimal states for learning in the home and in the classroom.**

The following lists provide sample activities in the move category. As mentioned earlier, we have included activities for all six ways of moving, but we recommend beginning with the heavy work options. Since the heavy work list is longest, we grouped it into two segments: one for use in homes and another for use in classrooms. Some heavy work activities can be used in both settings, but they are listed where they can be implemented most easily. Following the list of heavy work options, other heavy work activities are explained in more detail. Then last in this section is a list of "heavy work, up and down, front and back, upside down, crash and bump, and circles" activities.

CAUTION: Obviously, children need proper supervision while moving. Some children should not participate in certain types of movement activities. Consult your therapist or physician for proper precautions.

"HEAVY WORK" ACTIVITIES AT HOME:

- climbing a tree
- moving furniture
- lifting and moving firewood
- carrying groceries in from the car
- carrying a heavy box upstairs, to the basement, or to the other end of the house
- scrubbing the floor on hands and knees
- taking out the garbage
- vacuuming or sweeping
- digging in the garden
- playing "Partner Exercises" on the Alert Program audiotape (see Appendix)
- mountain climbing or hiking outdoors (or on an indoor rock climbing wall)
- climbing up a rope or ladder swing (or climbing on a "ropes course")
- wheelbarrow walking
- walking upstairs, two at a time
- popping therapy ball with both feet at the same time while lying on your back
- karate
- swimming laps
- backyard play equipment that provides heavy work (You can place a waterbed mattress filled with water on top of a tarp. Have fun jumping on it, pushing with arms or feet, etc.)
- bike riding
- crabwalking or other animal walks
- pulling a sled up a hill
- weight lifting or working out with pull-up bar in door frame

"HEAVY WORK" ACTIVITIES FOR CLASSROOMS:

- recess time: climbing or crossing the monkey bars, the rings, or other climbing structures
- stretching muscles or singing baseball's 7th inning stretch song, "Take Me Out to the Ballgame"
- pushing on walls while standing in line at school
- carrying heavy box to the office or on other school errands
- pulling a wagon or pushing a weighted grocery cart in preschool
- pulling on a bike innertube (store in backpack to keep handy whenever needed)
- doing chair push-ups (Place arms on either side of the chair. Scoot bottom away from the back of the chair. Try to straighten arms, lifting bottom off of the chair.)
- doing table push-ups (Stand next to a table. Place hands on the table and push up so feet lift off the floor.)
- sweeping or mopping the gymnasium floor or hallway floor with a big broom
- washing cafeteria tables
- carrying milk tray or pushing a cart filled with lunch boxes to the cafeteria
- erasing the chalkboards
- moving mats, equipment, or school furniture
- putting chairs on top of desks to prepare for floor cleaning at the end of the school day

Tug-of-war

Materials:
1 thick, long rope (about 8-20 feet for a group)
a soft area to play on such as grass or mats
a way to mark off a section of the grass or mats
Optional: towel or blanket

Here's How:
1. Tie a scarf (or other brightly colored cloth) to the middle of the rope. Mark an area on the grass or mats, approximately two to four feet wide. The middle of the rope should align with the middle of the two to four foot wide playing area.

2. Establish the ground rules: Either team can call "stop" at any time and both teams agree to comply immediately. Decide what other rules are needed to keep everyone safe, such as, "We agree to stop if anyone falls."

3. Divide the group into two teams. Each team stands on either side of the scarf, holding onto the rope.

4. The leader says, "Go." You guessed it! All start to pull in their direction to try to pull the middle of the rope over their edge of the playing area.

Things We've Noticed:
- Most of us are familiar with this game played by large groups with a rope. You can play the game also in pairs, using a towel or blanket instead of a rope.

- If you have concerns about students falling, you may want to play in a seated position on a soft surface (e.g., grass, mats, or on a bed). To avoid rope burns, children can wear work gloves.

- We get the most heavy work by long sustained pulling or by playing more than one tug-of-war game. We might want to encourage a more cooperative game, by timing how long both teams can pull without the other side falling over.

- Lots of long, low grunting and groaning while pulling adds breath support and adds to the fun!

39

Push-of-war

Materials:
2 children to work as a pair
1 large pillow per pair (a pillow from a bed or from a couch
  or a therapy ball)

Here's How:
1. Have children sit on the floor with their backs facing each other. Knees should be bent about 45 degrees.

2. Place a pillow or therapy ball between the children's backs.

3. An adult leader of the group says, "Push." Upon hearing the signal, each child pushes with her back as her partner does the same. Keep pushing until the "stop" signal is given.

4. Relax for a few seconds. Re-set the pillow and your posture. Repeat at least 3-5 times.

Things We've Noticed:
- This activity provides a lot of heavy work to muscles and joints. The pillow eliminates the problems of children poking or hurting each other inadvertently.

- Bending the knees allows children to push with more force against each other. Maintaining backs in a sitting position avoids strain on the back muscles. Obviously, any person with joint or muscle problems should not participate in this activity.

- Children can experiment by pushing with different body parts, such as pushing on the pillow or therapy ball with their hands while in a kneeling position.

- By not touching each other directly, many children who are sensitive to light touch can participate. Watch for the smiles and giggles.

Caterpillar Tunnel

Materials:
"Caterpillar" cloth tunnel is made of 3 yards or more of 18" cotton ribbing (available in fabric stores)

Here's How:
1. Lay Caterpillar Tunnel out lengthwise on floor.

2. At least one person holds the tunnel open or each end of the tunnel can be draped over an innertube.

3. All children crawl through the tunnel. Children can take turns holding the tunnel open for each other.

Things We've Noticed:
- This activity is adapted easily to suit many different learning situations. It is one of our favorite activities because the tunnel is not a bulky or expensive piece of equipment. It can be folded up and put away when not in use.

- Any type of task can be the "end product" for this activity (refer to the text of the Move! chapter of this book for a more detailed description of end products). As each child crawls through the tunnel, they need a moment to focus on a task to avoid the possibility of escalation. We found that end products could range from simple matching games to worksheets attached to clipboards. For example, for a matching game, place half of the cards at the beginning of the tunnel and the other half of the match at the end of the tunnel. The child picks up one card, crawls through the tunnel, then stops a moment to find the match at the end of the tunnel. For worksheets, place a clipboard with an appropriate page of work at the end of the tunnel. Each time the child crawls through the tunnel, he completes one or more problems and then repeats the sequence. This is a wonderful way to get periods of movement followed by periods of concentration which supports self-regulation and learning.

- Some therapists and parents use lycra or polyester materials for tunnels. While these materials are fine, we prefer the cotton ribbing with the highest percentage of cotton. It seems to require the most amount of heavy work while crawling. After being stretched by many children crawling through it, it's easy to wash. Dry it in a dryer so it will shrink back to its original size.

1. holder
6. holder
3. child crawling
4. puzzle
2. holder
5. holder

- Adults tend to look at the tunnel and worry about the tight, enclosed space. Most children are comfortable and even excited to crawl through the tunnel. If you find children concerned or fearful of the tunnel, try folding it until it is only one foot long. Then the "caterpillar" can grow as each child crawls through it, until children are enjoying crawling through the whole length of tunnel. Never force children to crawl through the tunnel. If they are apprehensive, ask them to be a "helper" to hold one end of the tunnel while others crawl through it. They will get plenty of heavy work until they feel ready to participate.

- The tunnel can be used successfully with an individual child or group of children. A group of children can learn to work with very little supervision once they've learned how to take turns holding and rotating positions. Let's take the example of working with six children, using a puzzle as the end product. Each child stands in one of the six positions. It is best to place pieces of paper with the numbers 1-6 written on them at each of the positions. (See illustration.) When you are in the number 3 position, you pick up a puzzle piece, crawl through the tunnel, and place the puzzle piece in the formboard at number 4 position. Meanwhile, all other children shift positions to the next number. The child at the number 1 positions goes to 2, 2 goes to 3, 3 goes to 4, 4 goes to 5, 5 goes to 6, and 6 goes to the number 1 position. Continue in this manner as long as children are enjoying themselves.

- Many children love the feeling of being "inside" the tunnel. Sometimes these children tease us and don't want to come out. You might want to help create a "getaway" space for these children in the classroom or home as mentioned in the next chapter (Touch!) of this book.

Isometrics

Materials:
none
NOTE: This activity can be done individually or as a group.
The group will need a leader.

Here's How:
1. In a seated position, place your palms together, imitating a position of praying. Push your palms against each other for a few seconds. (Leader would say, "Push.") Then relax for a few seconds. (Leader would say, "Relax.") Repeat 3-5 times. Remember we are going for lots of heavy work input to the joints and muscles, so decide on the number of repetitions accordingly.

2. Next, curl the fingers on each hand to form a semicircle. Rotate one hand toward your body and one hand away from your body. Interlock your fingers, imitating a position of an opera singer. Pull your elbows in the opposite directions while keeping your fingers interlocked for a few seconds. Relax for a few seconds and repeat at least 3-5 times. In the opera singer position, switch hands so the hand that was on top is now on the bottom. (Leader would continue throughout the steps of the isometrics to say, "Push and relax.")

3. Now raise both arms straight over your head. Clasp your hands and stretch upward for a few seconds, pretending you're touching the ceiling with your hands. Relax for a few seconds and repeat at least 3-5 times.

4. Then shrug your shoulders up close to your neck for a few seconds, pretending to touch your shoulders to your earlobes. Relax for a few seconds and repeat at least 3-5 times.

5. Next roll your neck and head slowly. Start by tucking your chin toward your right shoulder. Move head in a gentle sweeping motion to move your chin toward your chest and proceed until the chin is tucked toward your left shoulder. Pause a few seconds and reverse. Relax a few seconds and repeat 3-5 times.

6. Now place your right palm on top of your right knee. Try to push your knee up and push down with your hand, holding for a few seconds. Relax for a few seconds and repeat at least 3-5 times. Switch hands and knees and repeat this same sequence.

7. Finally, place one foot on top of the other. Try to push the bottom foot up and push the foot that is on top downwards. Do this for a few seconds. Relax for a few seconds and repeat for at least 3-5 times. Reverse the position of the feet and repeat this same sequence.

Things We've Noticed:

- While the number of steps listed above may seem lengthy, we've taught many students the sequence (in part or whole) and they learned it quite quickly.

- Some teachers use isometrics with the whole class. Others allow individual students to do this sequence by themselves whenever they need a break or perhaps just before a test.

- When teaching isometrics to an individual student, we emphasize the need to do the isometrics quietly, so as not to disturb others in class.

- At home, isometrics can be done anytime. Common times are at homework time, upon waking, and before bedtime.

Arm & Wrist "Pushes"

Materials:
none, just a group of children and a leader

Here's How:
1. Everyone stands shoulder to shoulder to form a line (or several lines, if there are many children).
2. Each person raises arms with <u>elbows bent</u> so that all are touching palm to palm.
3. On signal from the leader, each person pushes their palms against their neighbors' palms, trying to match the energy of how hard the neighbor is pushing.
4. On signal from the leader, all stop pushing and relax for a few seconds.
5. Start at step #3 and repeat at least three times, or as many times seems appropriate to provide the amount of heavy work engines need to get to the "just right" level.

Things We Noticed:
- This activity is a great pick when you know your group is able to be gentle and won't knock each over. With a little practice, most children can learn to do this and have fun.

- When forming a line, the people standing on the ends will have one arm that is not being pushed against. In order to prevent the feeling of "lopsidedness," the end person should turn 180 degrees, so that they use one arm for half of the repetitions and their other arm for the other half of the repetitions. If the leader directs six repetitions, after the third repetition, the leader tells the end people to switch. They turn and face the opposite direction of the line. The leader then directs the last three repetitions.

- If two people are going to do the Arm and Wrist "Pushes," they can stand facing each other and push, still using a signal or counting together saying, "Ready? Push 1,2,3. Relax. Push 1,2,3 . . . "

45

Arm & Wrist "Pulls"

Materials:
none, just a group of children and a leader

Here's How:
1. Everyone stands shoulder to shoulder to form a line (or several lines, if there are many children) as in the activity above.

2. Wrap your one hand around one of your neighbors' wrists and she will do likewise around your wrist. Then wrap your other hand around your other neighbor's wrist. Each of your hands should be overlapping each of your neighbor's wrists. Spread the line out to allow each person to stand with <u>elbows straight.</u>

3. On signal from the leader, the people on each end of the line gently lean away from the middle of the line, creating traction in shoulders, elbows, and wrists.

4. On signal from the leader, the people on each end of the line stop leaning away from the middle of the line, relaxing for a few seconds.

5. Start at step #3 and repeat at least three times, or as many times as seems appropriate to provide the amount of heavy work engines need to get to the "just right" level.

Things We've Noticed:
- As with the Arm and Wrist "Pushes," this is a great pick when you know your group is able to be gentle and they won't hurt each other's shoulders.

- The people in the middle of the line will experience the strongest pulling, so ask them to indicate if it is too much; then the people on the ends of the line can lean with less vigor. We have witnessed many people in the middle of the line, smile and utter a sigh of relaxation as they experience the positive effects of the traction.

- Also mentioned in the previous activity, when forming a line, the people standing on the ends will have one arm that is not pulled. In order to prevent the feeling of "lopsidedness," the end person should turn 180 degrees, so that they use one arm for half of the repetitions and their other arm for the other half of the repetitions.

- If two people are going to do the Arm and Wrist "Pulls," they can stand facing each other and pull, still using a signal or counting together saying, "Ready? Pull 1,2,3. Relax. Pull 1,2,3 . . . "

Shake Game

Materials:
None

Here's How:

1. With everyone standing, leader says, "Pretend you have a magic ball in your hands [hold imaginary ball with hands]. If we shake this ball, it will come alive [rapidly shake imaginary ball while children do the same]. And now we can move the 'shakes' into our heads [touch head for a moment, then shake head for about 5 seconds]. Good. Take the shakes out of your head and put them back into your hands [point to head, stop shaking head, then shake imaginary ball with hands]."

2. Leader repeats these types of instructions by placing the "shakes" into different body parts. For example, the leader could explain #1 above and then say, "Now let's put the shakes into our arms. Shake them up high, shake them down low, shake them up high again. Good. Now, put the shakes back into your hands [shake imaginary ball]. Can you find your hips? Put the shakes into your hips [shake hips]. Good. Now, take the shakes out, back in your hands. Hmmm… now let's put the shakes into our knees [shake knees]. Yes, let's wiggle our knees and wake them up. Now, back into your hands. Next, let's put the shakes into your feet. Go fast [march quickly], faster [march more quickly], slowly [lift knees up high slowly]. Great. Now put the shakes back into our hands again. Let's wake up our faces and voices. Put the shakes into your face and into your voices to make funny noises [quickly vibrate and rub hands on cheeks to make oohhs, aahhs, raspberry sounds with lips, high and low tones, etc.]. Very good [smiling]. Now, shakes back into our hands again."

3. The leader ends the activity by saying, "Let's put the shakes into our whole bodies. First, put some glue on your feet. Good. Now that we have glue on our feet, we can't run around the room, right? Put the shakes in your head, arms, hips, legs, faces, and voices [shake all body parts and make funny faces with sounds]. Wonderful! Now, let's put the shakes back into our hands. And guess what… the glue disappeared! Now, let's make the shakes disappear [keep shaking the imaginary ball]. Count with me…. 1…., 2…., 3…. and he shakes disappear! [slowly count aloud, raise your arms above head, then with a sweeping motion, bring arms to rest by side of body]."

4. Obviously, this is not an exact science! Many variations can be created such as: vary the body parts, vary the amount of time that each body parts shakes, ask children which body parts to shake, find unexpected body parts (like ribs or big toe).

NOTE: *A version of this activity was first taught by Irene Oliver Lewis as artist in residence with the Very Special Arts of New Mexico. Sincere thanks to her contributions to arts in New Mexico including arts education leader, playwright, actor, and co-founder of a charter high school in Las Cruces, NM.*

Pushing on Walls

Materials:
a firm wall (readily available in most homes and schools!)

Here's How:
1. Stand facing the wall with feet spread about shoulder length apart.
2. Place palms against the wall about shoulder height.
3. Lean body weight onto palms as you try to push the wall.
4. Relax and repeat as desired.

Things We've Noticed:
- Pushing on walls is a great heavy work movement break that can double as a "time killer" when there is an unexpected wait in line at school. Avoid the poking, pushing, and shoving that is often seen in lines by providing heavy work to the whole body.

- The variations abound: You can use different body parts to push against the wall. Some examples include pushing with the back, a shoulder, and lying on the floor to push with both feet.

- Wall push-ups are another variation of this activity. Face the wall with palms on the wall and feet slightly away from the wall as in the above description. Lean in so that your face almost touches the wall and elbows are bent. Then push back out to your original position. These push-ups are usually easy enough to make every-one feel strong. Remember that we can change the intensity of the push-ups by moving the position of our feet. Feet positioned far-ther from the wall require more intense arm muscle work. One-handed wall push-ups are another way to crank up the intensity.

Paper Sack Scoot ___ ___ ___

Materials:
1 paper grocery sack (folded to lay flat in a rectangle shape)
   per person
uncarpeted floor space
an empty container such as a bucket
bean bags (or a puzzle or other academic task)

Here's How:
1. Have child sit with his bottom positioned on the paper sack, knees bent and heels on the floor.

2. Have him pull by digging heels into the floor and flexing legs to move himself forward or push by pushing heels into the floor and extending legs. This will propel him backward.

3. Place bean bags at the beginning of the scooting path and a container at the end of the scooting path.

4. Provide the child with simple counting tasks, such as, "Take four bean bags down and put them in the container."

5. The child then takes one bean bag, puts it in his lap and scoots down to the bucket, comes back and repeats the sequence until he has the right number of bean bags in the container.

Things We've Noticed:
• We've provided a very simple cognitive task here. You can easily adapt this to many academic levels. You can keep the tasks simple such as a preschool puzzles (puzzle pieces at one end, formboard at the other end, and no container required). Or you can increase the difficulty by using flash cards for higher math problems, 3" x 5" cards with reading words or history questions on them, etc.

• The deluxe version of this game uses carpet samples (fuzzy side down) instead of paper grocery sacks.

Working under Pillows

Materials:
a few large, heavy pillows, or
a bean bag chair, or
some heavy blankets

Here's How:
1. Here's another example where the students get to teach us! Ask them if it might feel good to have some heavy pillows, or a bean bag chair, or some heavy blankets on top of them while they do their work.

2. Pile, pack around, or generally weight them down, checking that it feels good to them.

3. Choose an appropriate task for each child such as a doing a puzzle, reading a book, or completing paperwork. If you choose paperwork, you may want a clipboard for the worksheet.

4. Make sure that they have a signal to get out from under the pillows or that they're able to wiggle out when they're finished.

Things We've Noticed:
• This activity has many variations. One fun game is ask the child to lie down on a blanket and pretend that she is a "hot dog." We add mustard by giving extra deep touch and rubbing her arms and legs. Then add onions or relish in the same manner. Wrap the child up tight with the blanket (the hot dog bun), and then let her wiggle out. In the Southwest, we pretend to make burritos. You'll enjoy making up your own sandwiches, hamburgers and other fun things to eat. This activity has been a staple for many therapists for years. Let's have it spill over into homes and classrooms!

• Later in the Touch! chapter, you may notice the similarity of this activity to the story of a boy who was doing his math worksheet under a pile of pillows.

50

Seating Options

Materials:

Note: Having a variety of the following is best when trying to find what works for your students. If budgets are limited, try the beach ball or camping pillow. See the Appendix for a list of resources and suppliers.

Disco Sit   Camping Pillow
Move 'N Sit   Therapy Ball
Beach Ball   T-Stool

Here's How:

1. Seating options are designed to allow students the ability to make lots of subtle shifts in their posture while staying in their chair at home or school.

2. Allowing these frequent, subtle shifts can be very helpful for students who need movement to sustain their attention during seatwork.

3. Most students are able to use a seating option without disrupting others around them.

4. Students should not use the seating options all day, every day. It is recommended that teachers and parents develop a routine with their children so seating options can be used on an "as needed basis."

Things We've Noticed:

- As with many new items in a classroom, all the students may want to try the seating options at first, but eventually only those for whom they work will use them.

- The inexpensive beach ball and camping pillows are great low-budget options. To use the beach ball, barely inflate the ball. If you hear whoopee cushion noises, you've got too much air in it. The camping pillow can be used as a seating option when filled with air or a weighted lap pillow when filled with water.

- Allowing children to stand to do paperwork is a common, simple way to help children who need movement to focus. Most students won't want to stand for long periods of time, but allowing them the possibility can be important. Placing tape on the floor around a school desk helps some children better understand their personal space.

"Up & Down" Activities _____

- sitting on a teeter-totter or sitting on a rocking wooden boat in preschool
- jumping (just for fun or to music)
- doing jumping jacks
- jumping up to try to touch the top of a door frame
- jumping like an animal
- jumping rope
- playing hopscotch
- skipping
- sitting and bouncing on a therapy ball (see Appendix) while reciting the alphabet, practicing math facts or spelling words
- jumping on a trampoline
- trotting on a horse
- doing "The Wave" (as seen at sport arenas where the crowd alternates in standing, raising both arms at the same time, and then sitting down)
- sitting and bouncing on a hoppity hop
- standing and bouncing on a pogo stick
- spiking a volleyball
- dunking a basketball
- bouncing down a flight of stairs, sitting on your bottom
- marching to music
- Flash Card Jumping Game: Spread math flash cards on the floor in a path with an adequate distance between cards for jumping. Child rolls dice and jumps along the path, counting one number for each card to match the number rolled. Child stops and answers the problem on the flash card. Then rolls the dice again to continue. For younger children, the flash cards can be replaced with 5" x 8" cards. These cards can have colors, shapes, or other age-appropriate tasks written on them.

"Front & Back" Activities

NOTE: Running and other similar activities can be considered "front and back" movement. Technically, this is called "linear movement" because the inner ear perceives the body's forward and/or backward motion.

- swinging on a playground swing or backyard swing
- rocking in a rocking chair or on a rocking horse
- swinging on a front porch glider
- sitting on the floor with a partner, facing each other, feet touching, holding hands, and rocking back and forth
- sliding down a playground slide
- playing soccer
- ice skating
- roller blading
- sledding
- cross country and downhill skiing
- using seating options such as the inflatable camping pillow (see Appendix). When you place the camping pillow with the longest side perpendicular to the back of the chair, you can rock back and forth.

"Upside Down" Activities

- recess time: hanging by the knees on a playground bar with hands near the ground
- bending over with head between knees
- wheelbarrow walking
- lying over therapy ball on tummy or on back
- singing songs with upside down movements, such as "Heads Shoulders Knees and Toes" or "Do Your Ears Hang Low?"
- lying upside down over a sofa, padded arm chair, or beanbag chair
- rolling over a hassock or ottoman
- doing a head-stand starting from a "frog" three point position (In a squatting position, place hands on a carpeted floor or mat with forehead touching the carpet. Slowly roll knees onto bent elbows until balancing on forehead and hands. Try practicing head-stands near a wall for added balance.)

"Crash & Bump" Activities

NOTE: Glance through the activities listed below. Some children tend to bump into walls, door frames, or into other children, and even slam doors too hard, inadvertently. On the playground, these types of children may come running and crashing into you with a smile on their face. They are not intentionally trying to hurt you, but their bodies crave this type of impact. We say, "Oh. It looks like your body likes crashing into things, but my body doesn't want that right now. Let's try finding a safe way for your body to get some crashing and bumping." Children who crave crashing and bumping types of movement typically want intensity. Often they have difficulty finding safe ways to participate in "crash and bump" activities. Extra adult supervision is needed. Sometimes these types of children need occupational therapy in order to meet the intensity and types of movement their bodies are needing. Here are a few suggestions to try at home:

- jumping into a large pile of pillows
- jumping onto a track landing mat (You can make your own by buying a duvet cover or zippered mattress cover. Fill the cover with large pieces of foam. Upholstery stores often will donate used foam.)
- jumping into a pool, doing "cannon balls" into the pool, or jumping off a diving board
- jumping on an old mattress
- tackling while playing football
- driving bumper cars
- doing Extreme Sports, such as American Gladiators as seen on TV
- engaging in contact sports, such as ice hockey or rugby
- pillow fighting

"Circles" Activities

NOTE: We list this type of movement last because there is a higher probability that a child can "overload" or not process this movement properly. Consult with your occupational therapist to make sure your child is benefitting from spinning.

- sitting or standing on a merry-go-round
- sitting on a Sit n' Spin (available at Toys R' Us)
- standing and twirling
- spinning on a swing (could be an innertube or tire swing)
- spinning or twirling while dancing
- spinning while ice skating
- doing somersaults and tumbling in gymnastics
- doing cartwheels
- rolling in a large cardboard box or barrel (You can make your own barrel by covering a large round container with carpet.)
- sitting on a ferris wheel or other spinning amusement park rides
- rolling over a monkey bar or other bar on a playground
- lying over therapy ball ("circles") and plopping over into pillows ("crash and bump")
- flipping into a pool (sometimes called "watermelons")
- spinning in an office chair
- sliding down circular slides at a playground

Four

Touch!

TOUCH!

Have you ever tried to sit through a long conference? Imagine the feeling at about 4:00 pm when the conference is not over until 5:00 pm. What do normal adults do? We find a paperclip to destroy, or we start to tear off the label on our soda pop bottles, or we start to click our pen tops. Why do we do these things? Our nervous systems are trying to stay alert. Remember, without an appropriate sensory diet, the brain almost goes into sensory deprivation. In a conference room, no matter how interesting the speaker, eventually the novelty of the sensory environment wears off, causing you difficulty in attending. In addition, with limited movement while seated in the chair, your engine will probably go into a low state. Many of us rely on fidgeting and touching things to keep us alert in such a situation. Many children try to use the same tactile self-regulation strategies but often get into trouble. Better understanding of self-regulation is needed.

In this chapter, we will look at several considerations including fidgeting and holding objects, temperature variables, light touch, and deep touch. (A summary can be found in the *Leader's Guide*, page 2-9.) Along with each of these considerations, we will suggest activities and strategies that can be used before a task to prepare our engines, during the task to help us maintain alertness, or afterwards to prepare for the next task.

Quiet, Inexpensive, and Small Fidgets:

Fidgets are more acceptable in homes and schools when they are quiet, relatively inexpensive, and small. While fidgets that make noise are not "bad," they tend to limit where we are allowed to use them. We like to explain to children that it is the teacher's job to make sure everyone is learning. If one person disrupts another by making noise while fidgeting, the person with the loud fidget may need to find another quieter option to help his engine. Because fidgets are generally not the "highest quality" products, don't expect them to last a long time; they are in the "consumables" portion of school supplies just like pencils or glue. Choosing inexpensive toys can make it less frustrating when they wear out, deteriorate, break, or get lost. Small fidgets that can fit easily into a pocket, desk, or fanny pack are more readily available to us throughout the day. Since we all need help remaining alert and attentive at different times of the day and in different settings, portable fidgets are very helpful. Attaching fidgets to zippers of backpacks is currently popular. Also, we have heard of sewing fidgets or pieces of soft fabric (such as silk or velveteen) into a fanny pack. Gluing fabric swatches underneath a chair or inside of a school desk makes them handy for fidgeting but not disruptive to others.

Note: We will call items that you can use in the hand for self-regulation, "fidgets."

Novelty vs. Repetition

Sometimes the brain and nervous system seek novelty to stay alert. Just because a fidget works at one time of the day for a student, doesn't mean it will always work for that student. The need for novelty is why a fidget may seem to support self-regulation at first, but at another time of day or after a long period of use, stops being effective. Many teachers have a whole desk drawer full of fidgets they have taken away from children. If you take a fidget away from children who use fidgeting as a way to self-regulate, they will just find another one. They will even bring in rocks (for fidgeting) from the playground, if they have to!

In contrast, sometimes children seek repetition; their brains and bodies find comfort in doing the same thing, in the same manner, at the same time of day. For these children, offering the same fidget for self-regulation, for the same task, every day, supports their self-regulation. Some of these children will need to use the same fidget for an extended period of time. Once again, you can see that it will be a trial and error process; give a fidget to a child and see if it supports his engine (for which tasks, at which times of day, and for how long). Although we mention the need for novelty and/or repetition here in the Touch! chapter, the same principle applies in all sensorimotor categories.

Introducing Fidgets in Classrooms

Fidgets can be a bit more challenging strategy to introduce into a classroom than some of the heavy work strategies such as stretching or isometrics. We have found that teachers who use strategies in the touch category for their own self-regulation tend to be more comfortable allowing children the same opportunity. For example, if the teacher herself uses more strategies from the move category than from the touch category, she most likely will begin offering movement strategies first in her classroom. This is a fine plan because there are plenty of strategies in all of the categories for children to use for self-regulation. Our hope is that teachers will start using what they feel will work best for their group of students and then expand into other categories. In this way, children eventually will have a wide range of choices for their sensory diet.

Brain Toys

Teachers who feel comfortable offering fidgets for self-regulation have discovered ways to incorporate their use in the classroom. Just as "Brain Food" was mentioned earlier in the Put Something in the Mouth! chapter, teachers have found calling the fidgets, "Brain Toys" (Oetter, 1983) helps to differentiate them from regular toys. Some

teachers collect a variety of fidgets and place them in a basket. Over time students learn to choose fidgets that will help support their ability to focus. Teachers report that the basket is quite popular initially, but eventually only those students for whom fidgets are helpful will continue to use them. Some teachers offer the basket only for certain subjects in the day. Other teachers keep the basket on their desk and allow children to pick a fidget anytime in the day. Rather than the basket idea, some teachers prefer to have enough of the same fidget to pass out to everyone at the same time. For example, when the teacher is about to give a history lesson, she might explain, "Before I begin talking about Columbus, I'm going to pass out a bit of Silly Putty for everyone to use to help their engines. Remember the rules we talked about. I'm hoping that the putty will make it easier for us to learn about Columbus."

Now, some of you are thinking, "If I gave a fidget to Ruby, I know she would play with the fidget so much she would never pay attention!" Good for you. If you know this to be true, then don't give Ruby a fidget. Offer her another type of self-regulation strategy. But **let's not be too quick to determine that the fidget is not working for a child. We need to assess whether the strategy is working by observing its use.** For example, if a child is listening to an interesting history lesson and playing with her putty, ask the child a simple question about the content in a neutral tone of voice, "Ruby, do you remember what country Columbus came from?" If Ruby doesn't know, the child is not "wrong or bad," but her strategy for self-regulation is probably not working. We might say, "It looks to me like fidgeting with putty is not helping your engine right now. Would you like to try chewing on a piece of gum or on a straw?"

Fidgets in the Home
Fidgets may be easier to incorporate in the home than in the school setting. During homework time, on long car rides, while listening to a story read aloud, or while listening to a parent give instructions are all good times to try offering fidgets.

Luckily, fidgets are relatively popular right now and can be found fairly easily. Choose fidgets that are appropriate for the child's age, interests, and ability level. We have had great success looking in nature stores, such as Natural Wonders, The Discovery Store, or Store of Knowledge. Also, hospital and museum gift shops seem to have good collections of small toys. In stores like K-Mart, Walmart, and Target, don't forget to look in the "Party" sections for fidgets (See Appendix).

Some "Take Five" Fidget Suggestions
- Koosh balls (all varieties, some come as pencil toppers)
- relaxable balls (a common one looks like a world globe)
- small Slinky's or plastic coils
- coil shoe strings (the kind that do not require tying)
- drinking straws that are plastic with flexible necks for fidgeting
- colorful paperclips
- colored rubberbands
- plastic pop beads
- bendable animals and figures
- small Beanie Babies or other small stuffed animals
- Wikki Sticks (plastic wax strings)
- pipe cleaners
- hair scrunchies (fabric around elastic hair ties)
- rubber coiled keychains (the kind that can be worn on a wrist)
- "worry stones" or other smooth stones
- FiddleLink, a plastic triangle that is used typically in hand therapy (see Appendix for list of resources)
- pieces of soft fabrics such as silk or velveteen

Temperature Variables
Generally, neutral warmth or heat tend to be calming and relaxing to our bodies. Cool or cold temperatures tend to be more alerting. This certainly does not mean we should sit in a frigid, cold room to self-regulate, but temperature will affect our engine levels. For some, snuggled up in their bed under a pile of covers may not be a good place to try to study. For others, this may be the perfect place to complete homework.

At school, teachers are limited in how much they can control the temperature of their classrooms, but sometimes it is possible to open a window, allowing the fresh air in the room to create a more alerting environment. When environments are not at an ideal temperatures (too warm or too cool), we may need to use strategies from other categories to support students' ability to work efficiently.

At home, parents can help children to splash water or use a cold wash cloth on their faces as a "take five" break between pages of homework or to wake up more easily in the morning. At bedtime, parents can experiment with temperature by covering their children with lots of heavy blankets or just a light sheet. Also, experimenting with different types of sheets can help children self-regulate through the night, such as using flannel sheets, satin sheets, or sheets made of t-shirt material. Sleeping in a sleeping bag or on a waterbed that

Take note!
→

can be heated can be helpful strategies, too. Many of us have temperature preferences for bathing. Notice what is best for children's self-regulation: is it best for their state of alertness to take a hot bath before bedtime or a warm (even somewhat cool) shower upon rising?

Light and Deep Touch

The clothes we wear can give us light or deep touch input. This input can be one of the reasons we prefer certain types of clothing styles, textures, or fabrics. Children show us their sensorimotor preferences. Some like to wear baggy pants and others like tight fitting jeans (deep touch). Some prefer cotton sweatshirts while others prefer polyester turtlenecks. Parents may want to help children to experiment with a variety of clothing textures (e.g., soft, coarse, or silky), fabrics (e.g., knit, lycra, wool, or heavy cotton) and styles (e.g., loose fitting or snug). To receive deep touch throughout the day some children find it useful to wear silk or cotton long underwear, lycra exercise shorts, or tights under their clothing.

Many of us use light touch to help ourselves remain alert. Petting a dog or cat while reading may be just the right amount of light touch for us to continue reading and comprehending well. Light touch tends to be alerting, but there are exceptions. Some of us enjoy a light back scratch, with slow strokes up and down the back, as a way to wake up in the morning (alerting), while others enjoy this type of back scratch before we go to bed (calming).

Light touch such as tickling can be too much for some children's nervous systems; sometimes their brains and bodies perceive light touch or unexpected touch as painful, uncomfortable, or disconcerting. For these individuals, it is best to use deep (firm) touch and avoid unexpected touch (touch not seen from behind or in the periphery of their vision). The well-intentioned teacher or parent inadvertently can make children's engines go into high gear by just a pat on the back or shoulder (unexpected light touch). These types of children tend to not like fingerpaints, glue, or other gooey materials that involve light touch to their skin. Children who are hypersensitive to light touch cannot be "desensitized" by being forced to participate. Instead, they need occupational therapy to help their brains and bodies better interpret sensory information. At home or in the classroom, children who do not like light touch can be a "helper." Or, place the gooey material in a Ziploc bag, so the children can "play" without having to touch it. (See the Caution While Taking Five! Section in the Appendix.)

Deep touch is the "heavy work" of the touch category and can therefore help to either calm or alert the body. Some examples of deep touch are bear hugs, deep massage, or playing with a resistive putty. Wrestling and rough-housing are excellent ways to give children deep touch. Often we don't think of this type of play as calming, but parents have reported that rough-housing in the evening an hour or so before bedtime can be the perfect strategy to help children to fall asleep easily and stay asleep.

At home or school, parents and teachers can use touch strategies to help children's engines achieve optimal functioning. Parents can create a "getaway" space in the home by simply placing a blanket over a table or piling pillows in a corner of the children's bedroom. Some teachers create a reading corner, where children can lean into pillows, cover up with blankets, or hold a stuffed animal while they read. One teacher called this a "cozy corner" (Rodriguez, 1999), using beanbag chairs and pillows. Creating a cozy corner at home or school makes it possible for children to learn that they can calm their own engines by using touch and quiet. Another teacher (Keesley, 1995) used deep touch in her classroom to help children complete their work. When we first observed this activity, we were quite surprised to see a pile of pillows on the floor, but no child. As we watched, we could see the pile of pillows rise slightly, a hand come out, and the roll of two dice. Then the pillows dropped until a few seconds later when the pillows rose again. We found out that the child was doing his math worksheet under the pile of pillows! With the deep touch of the pillows on his body, this child's engine was running "just right" for the task.

A pile of pillows is an inexpensive way to use weight to provide deep touch at school or home. Home-made pillows can be stuffed with hosiery or other heavy material. Commercial products available include weighted vests and weighted blankets. (See Appendix for a list of resources.)

"Take Five" Deep Touch and Heavy Work Suggestions
- bee's wax (available at many natural food stores)
- Silly Putty or other oil based clays that do not dry out
- art erasers or putty that mounts posters on walls
- stuffed animals (Rip out part of the seam and insert a Ziploc bag of rice or other heavy, non-toxic weighted material.)
- "feely buckets" (Fill a dishpan with raw pinto beans in which to hide objects or Concentration game cards. Caution: Because beans fit nicely into nostrils, extra adult supervision is necessary.)
- lotion (Older children can keep a small container in their backpacks.)

- flour balloon (Make your own by filling a deflated, size 11" or larger helium balloon with flour, tie off the top, and fidget away!)
- Nickelodeon's Gak or Floam (available at Toys R' Us or other toy stores)
- make your own gooey substances with recipes from books like *MudWorks* or *Gook Book* (See Appendix for list of resources.)

Be creative and add to the list what you think will be supportive to the children with whom you live or work.

Five

Look!

LOOK!

When thinking of ways to support children's learning, the environment will be an important consideration. The visual input in the environment significantly affects our ability to attain, maintain, and change our levels of alertness. **In general, dim lighting, muted colors, and plain walls can be calming. On the other hand, bright lighting, lots of colors, and variety tends to be alerting.**

For example, some people create home and work settings that are bright, colorful, and full of visual stimulation. Others prefer a setting that is more cave-like with dim lights and very little color. Perhaps you have visited a classroom that is full of visual input. Every inch of wall space is covered in reds, yellows, and blues, bulletin boards are filled with posters, and cheery artwork is hung from the ceiling. In contrast, there are classrooms where a few cursive letters are posted above the chalkboard and the fire exit plan is on the bulletin board, and that's all there is for visual input. Neither of these classrooms is good or bad, right or wrong. We just want to point out that usually it's the teachers and parents who set up these environments, and the amount of visual stimulation will probably not fit all children's needs, all of the time. Since as adults we have most of the control of environments, it is important to watch for what supports children and what interferes with their functioning. Being aware of how visual input affects our ability to stay alert will guide us in choosing visual activities and creating optimal environments for learning.

Another issue in considering choices in the look category is the degree to which one is distracted visually. For example, some of us might be called "pile people." (If you are one, it's okay to admit it.) "Pile people" keep everything out on top of their desks, and if they don't, they forget they have work to do. And then there are the "non-pile" people, those who like their desk to be completely clear of any and all clutter. They would not be able to complete a single task on a desk piled high with papers. Now what's interesting is that the pile people insist that they can work and prefer to work with lots of papers surrounding them, but non-pile people don't believe this to be true. And the worst is when the non-pile people try to help the pile people by restacking their piles! Perhaps a non-pile person, who lived with a pile person, invented the roll-top desk for this very reason.

At School

It all comes down to our sensorimotor preferences: What do we prefer in our visual environment that helps us to concentrate, and what is visually distracting or interferes with our ability to concentrate? What

do we do if a fifth grade teacher, whose engine is in low gear after lunch, needs the lights on and all the window shades open wide to help her to stay alert, but the children whose engines are in high gear need to have dim lighting to calm down? Assuming the students already understand the Alert Program concepts, the teacher could talk about her engine and ask for the students' input. She might say, "I'm noticing that now after lunch my engine is in low gear. It's going to be hard for me to concentrate on reading the Harry Potter chapter aloud to you. To help my low engine, I'd like to open the blinds and brighten the room, but it looks like a lot of your engines are in high right now. Usually dimming the lights, helps engines that are in high gear. Anybody have any suggestions?" Someone might suggest that they use a strategy from another category or one that involves heavy work, because we know that heavy work helps when engines are in low OR high gear. Some options could include:

1) the teacher dimming the lights to help the students' engines, but using another strategy for her own engine such as chewing gum (heavy work in her mouth) or fidgeting with an art eraser (heavy work to her hand), or

2) the teacher and all students doing isometrics (heavy work to their muscles) before the story is read. (See activity page describing isometrics in the Move! chapter.)

In order to teach self-regulation, it is critical that the adults discuss their own levels of alertness and their own needs for sensorimotor strategies. When the teacher problem-solves with her students, they all learn more about themselves and how to respectfully cooperate with one another.

At Home

Parents also can adapt environments visually, helping children create bedrooms and study spaces that meet their sensorimotor preferences. Consider the kind and the amount of lighting: full direct sunlight through a window; bright light from a table lamp; or a dimmed, reflected torche pole lamp. One child described his bedroom enthusiastically to us. He said that he felt so lucky that his bedroom was the only room in the house with no windows. Clearly, a cave-like, dim environment was perfect for his engine, but we doubt he understood that not many other family members would be fighting him for the space!

In addition to visual environments, some children like to "take five" with toys that have a visual element. Oil and water toys such as glitter wands can be bought or made. Lava lamps have made a come-back since the 1960's. Buying a fish tank for a classroom or bedroom is a nice option. Many children even like the popular "fake aquariums" with plastic fish that move in the tank.

Full Spectrum Lighting

One final note about lighting: Some children and adults are sensitive to fluorescent light bulbs which have a hum when lit and often flicker. Full spectrum lighting is a welcomed alternative, providing a more natural type of light. (See Appendix for a list of resources.) Parents can replace fluorescent light bulbs with full spectrum lights or use incandescent lighting for study areas in the home. Teachers' options are often more limited, but many teachers have replaced fluorescent lighting with lamps in classrooms. (Check with your administrator regarding fire regulations.) The lighting in schools and other environments, such as large wholesale warehouses can be irritating to some children. These children may want to wear baseball hats or sunglasses for shading of the eyes.

In this chapter, we have presented a brief overview of the effects of visual input on self-regulation. We can't always modify the visual environment, but it is important to help children, their parents, and school staff to understand its impact on levels of alertness. Readers who want to learn more may want to consult local professionals trained in vision therapy, such as developmental optometrists, and those trained in sensory processing theory, such as occupational therapists.

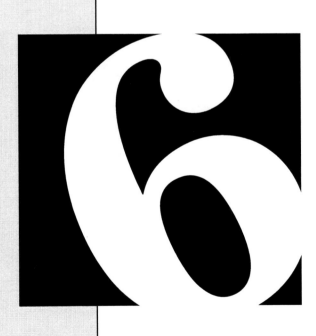

Six

Listen!

LISTEN!

Listen is the fifth category of ways to "take five." As we did in the Look! chapter, we will focus on the environment. Some of us learn best when we are in a quiet setting. Others function best in an auditorily stimulating environment. Our goal is to find just the right amount of sound and to understand what types, when, and with what intensity sounds affect our nervous systems.

Pause as you read this book. What do you hear? What sounds are in the background of your sensory environment? If you are reading this in your home, do you hear music from a radio or sounds from a TV, the hum of a refrigerator or clanging of plates shifting in the dishwasher, cars outside on the street, birds chirping, or children playing? Usually while reading, you are able to disregard or ignore many sounds so you can concentrate. Some children's (and adults') brains are not able to adequately block out the irrelevant sounds in the environment. They are distracted by the numerous background noises so much that they have difficulty concentrating or even functioning.

Some people need auditory input in order to concentrate; for these types of nervous systems, to try to read a book in a library or quiet room in their house would be counterproductive. They might prefer to read this book at a coffeehouse where there is plenty of background noise such as the coffee grinders running, utensils clanging, people talking, and jazzy music playing to keep engines running "just right."

In general, sounds that are most alerting are ones that are arrhythmical, of short duration, loud, or novel. Sounds that are calming and easiest for the nervous system to ignore, are ones that are rhythmical (in predictable patterns), of long duration, quiet, and familiar. Sirens from ambulances and fire trucks alert us because they are unique, unusual, and loud. If sirens were quiet, rhythmical, in predictable patterns, or familiar to us, they would not be effective warnings.

Usually, adults automatically adjust to sounds in their environment. Without even thinking about it, we might turn on the radio while we are balancing our checkbook, change a radio station to classical music to fall asleep at night, or turn off the radio in the car when we need to parallel park on a busy street. Some people automatically turn on loud rock n' roll music to clean the house; they are using music (auditory input) to change their level of alertness to get pumped up. Children are not as automatic in their understanding of how auditory input affects their level of alertness. They may need adults to help teach them what sounds support their self-regulation and what sounds are distracting or irritating to them.

Music

Frequently, music is used to support self-regulation. In both home and school settings, listening to music while we work, or "taking five" away from the work, can affect our levels of alertness. Parents and teachers can help children experiment and then determine which type of music supports their self-regulation. Try a wide range of music and watch individual reactions to classical, country western, chanting, Native American drumming, easy listening, folk, instrumental, international music, jazz, Latin, marches, nature sounds, New Age, opera, pop, punk, rap & hip-hop, rhythm & blues, rock n' roll, show tunes, and sound tracks.

For example, upon rising, parents can try various types of music to see which best helps the children awaken. They may start off playing classical music quietly and then increase the volume, perhaps switching to rock n' roll to alert the children. At school, after lunch recess when children's engines are in high gear, teachers can use the low, deep pitch of a Native American drum to help children to self-regulate. As children enter the room, teachers can beat on the drum, beginning with a steady, quick rhythm to match the children's level of alertness. Then the teacher can slow down the beat of the drum to help children's engines get to a "just right" range for the next task of the day.

At our "How Does Your Engine Run?"® conferences we do a demonstration using music. We ask participants to read to themselves two pages from their handouts in preparation for small group discussions. We play music quietly while participants are reading the material. After several minutes, we ask participants whether or not the music supported their ability to remain alert. No matter what type of music we try, we have never had more than 50% agreement among groups. Some participants adamantly suggest their favorite type of music, but one type of music never works for everyone. Teachers in classrooms may have the same difficulty finding consensus regarding what type of music to play, at what time of day, and at what volume to support self-regulation. Trial and error, however, can be educational in and of itself, if teachers allow the children to be part of the process.

Creating Environments in the Listen Category

Adults can assist children to adapt auditorally to environments, creating spaces at home (bedrooms or study spaces) and at school ("getaway" spaces or "cozy corners" as described in the Touch! chapter). Linda Hydar, a teacher, came up with an ingenious way to deal with these differing preferences for the amount of noise in our environments. She explained to her class that some people like city life where there is lots of noise and commotion. Others prefer country life where there is less noise and commotion. She divides her classroom into these two types of environments and encourages children to move their desks into either the city or the country, depending on how much auditory input they need or want. "It is not at all a chaotic situation in my room because many children who make a choice find that the choice they make fits their learning style and want to remain in the city or country because it feels comfortable for them. My goal is to help them realize that everyone learns differently and [I] want them to be able to realize the best learning environment for them[selves]." This teacher is helping children to learn what adults usually do automatically to accommodate to noises in the environment. In addition, the children have the added benefit of heavy work to their muscles and joints when moving their desks to the different parts of the classroom.

What Sounds Support Or Bother Engines?

Teachers and parents need to assist children to understand what sounds in the environment help their engines and what sounds bother their engines. For example, if there is a fire drill, teachers can help children observe how their engines probably go into high as a result of the fire bell. For a few children, whose reaction is extreme, it may be necessary to warn them ahead of time that the fire bell will be ringing and help them to prepare or avoid the sound all together. (See Caution While Taking Five section of the Appendix.) Eventually, many who are auditorally sensitive can learn to predict that if they enter a noisy environment, their engines may go into high. For example, school cafeterias are often a nightmare for children who are sensitive to sounds. Teachers may suggest that children at lunch wear earplugs, listen to music through headphones, or better yet, request to eat in a quiet room instead (with a friend and adult supervision). When children are doing seatwork or taking a test, teachers can give the verbal directions and then allow children to use earplugs or headphones, so they are not distracted by the sounds in the classroom.

White Noise

White noise is a type of sound that provides a filter for the listener. White noise machines often have recordings of sounds, such as rain or ocean waves, to drown out other disruptive background noises. Indoor waterfalls, fans, or aquarium air pump motors are other forms of white noise. Children sometimes create their own form of white noise by humming or making their own sounds to block out annoying background noises. For self-regulation or for white noise, when one person wants music and when another person prefers quiet, the use of portable audio players can be helpful. In this same vein, teachers can set up listening centers with headsets so children can listen to different types of music.

Most of our work and home environments are becoming filled with more and more distracting noises (e.g., ringing of phones and fax machines, buzzing from computers and printers, or humming from heaters and air conditioners). With more sounds in our environments, it is essential to help children understand how sounds affect their engines and how to "take five."

CAUTION: Loud noises can damage ears and cause permanent hearing loss! Consult with an audiologist for proper precautions.

72

Seven

In Closing . . .

IN CLOSING . . .

We hope that this book has helped you to gain insight into self-regulation and to expand the number of options to support children's learning. By "taking five," we all can learn to better adjust and maintain optimal alertness in the tasks of our daily lives. Understanding the importance of self-regulation benefits us all.

Learning to cooperate and negotiate the differences in our sensory diet preferences is a life skill. Most of us unconsciously assume "what I prefer is what you prefer." It goes against our somewhat self-centered belief system to try to understand that what I need to self-regulate is not the same as what you need. After we embrace that assumption, then we can understand our officemates, family members, and fellow students. In a way, it helps us to accept diversity and look outside ourselves to accommodate for others' sensorimotor needs. Many arguments with our loved ones could be avoided if we better understood what sensorimotor strategies we all employ to stay alert throughout the day. We also might have greater understanding, tolerance, and appreciation for the children with whom we live and work.

We believe all behavior has meaning and that it is our job as parents and teachers to seek out what children might be communicating to us through their behavior. Too many times self-regulation behaviors are misinterpreted negatively. Not all behaviors can be attributed to self-regulation strategies, but let us not overlook how many are.

my engine . . .

We would like to close by sharing one final, true story about a typical day in the life of a special four-year-old, Mark. This child was fortunate to have a supportive team who worked together to create the right formula for his success. By using the *Take Five!* strategies, Mark's engine is supported to be in an optimal state for home and school activities. Mark's story illustrates how **we all need a variety of strategies to attain, change, and maintain different levels of alertness for different tasks throughout the day.** We hope Mark's story will inspire you as much as it inspires us.

Mark attends a full-day, regular education kindergarten. When we met his parents at one of our "How Does Your Engine Run?"® conferences, Mark had just been evaluated by an occupational therapist (OT). The evaluation showed signs of sensory processing problems that were most evident in his difficulties in making transitions from one activity to another, in behavioral outbursts (especially with unexpected light touch and in noisy environments), and poor self-regulation. At the conference, Mark's parents learned about engine

73

levels and sensorimotor strategies. Together, with the help of his school OT, Mark's parents developed a daily routine that has significantly improved his ability to make transitions, decreased the number of behavioral outbursts, and increased his ability to self-regulate at home and school.

Mark now wakes up in the morning and eats breakfast while listening to the music from the "Mozart for Modulation" CD (Frick & Richter, 1998). Then it's time to get dressed for school. Mark likes to wear a soft, satin, short-sleeved T-shirt under his clothing. After teethbrushing and haircombing, Mark's mother rolls him up tightly into a blanket to give his body a deep squeeze (deep touch input). Mark likes to watch the TV show, Arthur. While watching the first half of Arthur, Mark enjoys a specific regimen (Wilbarger & Wilbarger, 1991-2001); after a special type of touch, he helps his mom count up to ten as she pushes and pulls each joint of his body (from his toes, up to his shoulders and neck). For the second half of the Arthur show, Mark picks one heavy work activity from a list of his favorites. He might pick crabwalking or wheelbarrow walking across the room with his siblings. Or he might pick a version of London Bridges, in which Mark and his siblings sing the song while he pushes against the wall. When they get to the "they all fall down" part, Mark falls onto one of his siblings with lots of giggles.

Next the bus takes Mark to school where he greets his teacher who also has been learning about engines and the need to "take five." Mark's teacher has a basket of fidgets on her desk and a container of gum. Even though Mark's teacher does not allow gum for her other students, she was willing to have Mark try using gum to keep his engine running "just right." The adults were a bit apprehensive how the other children would respond. Mark came home one day and reported to his mother that another girl in the class asked him why he got to chew gum. Mark, without prior coaching, simply explained, "I need to chew gum because it helps me to focus." The girl was convinced and there were no problems with the use of gum.

At lunch time, Mark goes to the cafeteria with his classmates. His mother packs him either a crunchy or chewy snack or a straw for sucking up applesauce or pudding. His friends have caught on to this, and they like to try sucking up their pudding with a straw, too.

After-lunch recess used to be a challenging time for Mark. The transition from outside recess to coming into the class made his engine go quickly into high gear and he often had behavior "melt downs." His OT suggested to the teacher that Mark carry a backpack (heavy work). Mark loved to be his teacher's helper and carry her books. When the OT consulted again, she realized that the backpack was too heavy for Mark's size and age, so she recommended he try a weighted vest. It was explained to Mark that he could wear the vest to "help build up his muscles." Times of transition are much easier now, including after-lunch recess and going to/from art class, music class, the library, and the cafeteria. Mark is comfortable with this routine; when he leaves the classroom he puts on his vest and when he enters the next room, he has his own hook to hang up his vest until he leaves the room again. Over time, wearing a vest has become somewhat of a "status symbol" in the classroom. Many children like to wear "regular" vests just as Mark does!

At rest time, Mark goes to his teacher's desk to pick an item from the basket. He chooses between a relaxable ball, a fidget he calls his "squeezy" dog, or his rainbow string pipe (see Appendix). He can rest quietly with the others while he uses his fidget or blows on his pipe.

Typically, on the bus ride home, Mark sleeps after a full day of fun. When he returns home, his parents observe him to determine if his engine needs to "take five, fifteen, or fifty!" He usually watches TV a bit after school with his siblings while bouncing on his large therapy ball (see Appendix) or jumping on his trampoline.

Next, it's time for dinner. Mark sits on a Disco Sit seating option (see Appendix) to help him to converse more easily and eat at the dinner table. After a busy day, Mark takes a bath where he gets a special rub down with a sponge. In his bedroom, he falls asleep by watching his lava lamp in the dark.

In addition to his sensory diet, Mark receives OT twice weekly to remediate his sensory processing difficulties. Also, he attends a "Get Along Gang" group facilitated by the school counselor to support his social skill development.

This peek into Mark's daily routine shows how his parents, teacher, and OT have developed the right sensorimotor formula for his brain and body to function best. Some children may need more strategies and more intensity. Other children may need fewer strategies and less intensity.

We will end with the wisdom of this young boy. Mark was in the library with his classmate one day. As he often does, he was using his fidget to help his engine stay "just right." Mark watched another boy run frantically around the library. After a few minutes, Mark walked up to the other boy and said, "Your engine is on high. Here, use my fidget. It will help." Our hope is that as we all learn the benefits of "taking five," we can be as kind and generous with our knowledge as Mark.

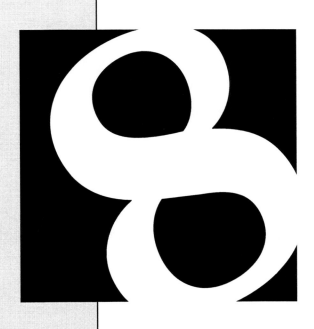

Eight

Appendix

CAUTION while "Taking Five!"

Normally developing children experience the "joyful exploration of sensation" (Wilbarger, 1991-2001). Some children are more cautious than others, but when children seem fearful, especially in new situations, in times of transition, or when exploring new materials, we want to rule out the possibility of an underlying problem. Professionals trained in sensory processing theory and treatment can identify possible causes. Some children require occupational therapy or other professional help to address their needs and help them feel "comfort, safety, confidence, and competence" (Oetter, 1987).

Children who experience the world as unsafe, alarming, or irritating due to the way in which their brains misinterpret the sensory input in their environments may have sensory defensiveness. One of the brain's main jobs is to protect the body. "Sensory defensiveness is simply the overactivation of our protective senses. It is a misperception that makes our clothes feel like spiders on our skin and stairs seem like cliffs. . . . Common symptoms may include over sensitivity to light or unexpected touch, sudden movement or over reaction to unstable surfaces, high frequency noises, excesses of noise or visual stimuli, and certain smells" (Wilbarger & Wilbarger, 1991).

Any nervous system will respond to protect the body if the brain's perception is that of danger. To an observer, this reaction may seem extreme, but the brain's first priority is protection of the body. Therefore, a real threat or perceived threat (based on past or present experience) is handled in the same way. A perceived threat is real to the perceiver, and it needs to be honored as her truth. As parents and teachers, we must honor children's perception of their sensorimotor world and respect their needs.

Children who are sensory defensive cannot be "desensitized" by being forced to participate in activities that their nervous system perceives as dangerous or irritating. These children need our understanding and support. Their engines quickly can go into high gear and sometimes go over the edge when their brains try to shut out the sensory bombardment completely; their engines may look like they are in a low level of alertness, when truly their nervous systems are shut down. This is a serious condition of the nervous system. Children who have sensory defensiveness can rapidly go into this shutdown state.

Watch for symptoms of sensory defensiveness. If you observe this type of reaction to any sensory input (from what they see, feel, taste, touch, smell, or certain types of movement), ask an occupational

therapist or other professional trained in sensory processing theory and treatment for an evaluation and recommendations. Occupational therapists can treat sensory defensiveness with a specific regimen (Wilbarger's Protocol with deep touch pressure followed by joint compression) to remediate the underlying problem (Wilbarger & Wilbarger, 1991-2001). However, also using a sensory diet throughout the day and other sensorimotor strategies from *Take Five!* will help during and after treatment. If you want to learn more about sensory defensiveness, refer to the Appendix to find a list of references and resources.

If you observe children having any type of difficulty with the *Take Five!* activities or you are concerned for their safety, stop the activity and seek consultation from a professional. As with any advice or suggestions regarding children, it is the adults' responsibility to provide a safe, properly supervised environment. TherapyWorks, Inc. cannot be responsible for negligent or improper use of these activities. Our hope is that all will safely enjoy and benefit from the *Take Five!* suggestions.

OTHER ALERT PROGRAM PRODUCTS

LEADER'S GUIDE BOOK
This book is the "original" and explains the Alert Program® in its entirety. It guides you through the 12 steps to teach independent self-regulation with an extensive list of activities and clinical stories. The book includes all worksheets needed for the program.

INTRODUCTORY BOOKLET
This booklet is our ol' faithful way of sharing the basics of the Alert Program with those who may not be familiar with its concepts. Readers of this booklet will be more prepared to support children's use of the engine analogy and self-regulation strategies.

TEST DRIVE BOOK/CD
This book, and accompanying CD with its appealing songs, is the fastest way of teaching the Alert Program to children (and adults). The book is full of practical ideas to show you how to use the songs, step-by-step, in classroom, homes, and therapy clinics.

ALERT: GO FISH! AND ALERT BINGO
These printable card games are available to print directly to your home printer. These outstanding Go Fish and Bingo game variations effort-lessly teach children the basics of the Alert Program.

KEEPING ON TRACK: Alert Program Companion Game
This board game reinforces the Alert Program concepts. The visually engaging road trip includes game instructions and "bonus material" with plenty of tips to make the game successful for children of different ability levels.

ALERT PROGRAM CD
This double CD set includes an introduction to the program read by the authors. The playful songs are coded for increasing or decreasing alert levels. (Note: these songs do not use the "engine analogy." The *Test Drive* songs teach self-regulation through the engine vocabulary.)

CEU CREDIT FOR JUST READING
Learn more about how you can earn CEU credits for reading our Alert Program products at www.AlertProgram.com.

NOTE: Some people believe that they need all the products in order to use the program. Actually, the Leader's Guide is the only product that is essential for implementing the whole program. But many don't have time to teach the whole program with all its steps and stages, so instead they start with the Test Drive book and CD, Introductory Booklet, Take Five! book, or Alert Program CD. It's up to you! (Go to www.AlertProgram.com to learn more).

REFERENCES

Frick, S., & Richter, J. (1998). <u>Mozart for modulation selections to enhance attention and learning.</u> [CD]. Hugo, MN: PDP Press.

Frick, S., Frick, R., Oetter, P., & Richter, E. (1996). <u>Out of the mouth of babes: Discovering the developmental significance of the mouth.</u> Hugo, MN: PDP Press.

Keesley, E. (1995). Personal communication. Gallup, NM.

Oetter, P. (1983). <u>Sensory Integration Treatment Course.</u> Paper presented for Professional Development Programs, multiple locations.

Oetter, P. & StevensDominguez, M. (1989). <u>Project ASK.</u> Technical Assistance Unit, UAP, University of New Mexico, Albuquerque, NM.

Oetter, P. (1991). Sensorimotor planning worksheet. In M.S. Williams & S. Shellenberger (Eds.), <u>"How Does Your Engine Run? A Leader's Guide to the Alert Program for Self-Regulation.</u> Albuquerque, NM: TherapyWorks. (pp1-14).

Oetter, P., Richter, E., & Frick, S. (1995). <u>MORE: Integrating the mouth with sensory and postural functions.</u> Hugo, MN: PDP Press.

Rodriguez, J. (1999). Personal communication. Albuquerque, NM.

Sensory Integration International (1991). <u>Caution: Children at work.</u> The Ayres Clinic at Sensory Integration International.

Wilbarger, P. (1984). Planning an adequate sensory diet: Application of sensory processing theory during the first year of life: <u>Zero to Three,</u> V(1), 7-12.

Wilbarger, P., & Wilbarger, J. (1991-2001). <u>Sensory defensiveness and related social/emotional and neurological problems.</u> [Workshop at multiple locations].

Wilbarger, P., & Wilbarger, J. (1991). <u>Sensory defensiveness in children ages two to twelve: an intervention guide for parents and other caretakers.</u> Van Nuys, CA: Avanti Educational Programs.

Wilbarger, P. (1995). The Sensory Diet: Activity programs based on sensory processing theory. <u>Sensory Integration Special Interest Section Newsletter.</u> Bethesda, MD: American Occupational Therapy Association, 18 (2), 1-4.

Williams, M. S., & Shellenberger, S. A. (1992). <u>An introduction to "How does your engine run?" the alert program for self-regulation.</u> [Introductory Booklet]. Albuquerque, NM: TherapyWorks.

Williams, M. S. & Shellenberger, S. A. (1994). <u>The alert program with songs for self-regulation.</u> [double CD set]. Albuquerque, NM: TherapyWorks.

Williams, M. S., & Shellenberger, S. A. (1996). <u>"How does your engine run?" A leader's guide to the alert program for self-regulation.</u> [Leader's Guide]. Albuquerque, NM: TherapyWorks.

RESOURCES

The following are organizations, therapy supply companies, or conference coordinators. The specific items we mentioned in the text are coded for easy reference. Match the number of the item you wish to purchase with the company below:

Camping pillow seating option (Intex) (12)
Disinfecting solution for cleaning whistles (10)
Disc O' Sit seating option (10, 16)
FiddleLink (16)
Fidgets (8, 9, 10, 16)
Full spectrum lighting (11)
Gook Book (9)
Harmonicas, kazoos, and siren whistles (10, 16)
Move' N Sit seating option(10, 15, 16)
Mudworks (see List of Additional Reading)
Rainbow string pipe (10)
Relaxable balls (8, 10, 16)
Related Continuing Education Courses (1, 2, 4, 5, 6, 7, 10, 14, 17)
SITFIT seating option (10, 16)
T-Stool (15)
Therapy balls (3, 10, 13, 15, 16)
Theratubing (10, 13, 15, 16)
Weighted vests, blankets and other weighted items (13, 15, 16, 18)

1) American Occupational Therapy Association, Inc.
   4720 Montgomery Lane
   PO Box 31220
   Bethesda, MD 20824-1220
   phone: 1-800-SAY-AOTA
   fax: 1-301-652-7711
   www.aota.org

2) Avanti Educational Programs, Inc.
   315 Meigs Road, # 288
   Santa Barbara, CA 93109
   phone: 1-800-405-8942
   fax: 1-805-319-0715
   www.avanti-ed.com

3) Ball Dynamics International, Inc.
   14215 Mead Street
   Longmont, CO 80504
   phone: 1-800-752-2255
   www.balldynamics.com

4) Belle Curve Records, Inc.
   C/o Future Horizons
   721 W. Abram Street
   Arlington, TX 76013
   phone: 1-800-489-0727
   fax: 817-277-2270
   www.fhautism.com

5) Developmental Concepts-
   Ready Approach
   (taught by Laura Barker)
   33565 Nancy Street
   Livonia, MI 48150
   phone: 734-516-4009
   fax: 734-422-0051
   www.sensoryprocessing.com

6) Developmental Delay Resources (DDR)
   5801 Beacon Street
   Pittsburgh, PA 15217
   phone: 800-497-0944
   fax: 412-422-1374
   www.devdelay.org

7) Learning Disabilities Association
   of America (LDA)
   4156 Library Road
   Pittsburgh, PA 15234-1349
   phone: 412-341-1515
   fax: 412-344-0224
   www.ldanatl.org

8) Oriental Trading Company
   P.O. Box 2308
   Omaha, NE 68103-2308
   phone: 1-800-875-8480
   fax: 1-800-327-8904
   www.orientaltrading.com

9) Pocket Full of Therapy
   P.O. Box 174
   Morganville, NJ 07751
   phone: 800-pfot-124
   fax: 732-441-1422
   www.pfot.com

10) Professional Development Programs (PDP)
    1675 Greeley Street South Suite 101
    Stillwater, MN 55082
    phone: 651-439-8865
    fax: 651-439-0421
    www.pdppro.com

11) Play Clay Factory
    217 S. Main Street
    Lamar, CO 81052-2832
    phone for orders: 1-800-925-2529
    phone for information: 719-336-3526
    www.playclayfactory.com

12) REI or Brands on Sale at
    www.brandsonsale.com
    www.rei.com

13) Sammons Preston
    P.O. Box 5071
    Bolingbrook, IL 60440-5071
    phone: 1-800-323-5547
    fax: 1-800-547-4333
    www.sammonspreston.com

14) SPD Foundation
    5655 S. Yosemite Suite 305
    Greenwood Village, CO 80111
    phone: 303-794-1182
    fax: 303-322-5550
    www.spdfoundation.net

15) Southpaw Enterprises, Inc.
PO Box 1047
Dayton, OH 45401
phone: 1-800-228-1698
fax: 937-252-8502
www.southpawenterprises.com

16) Therapro, Inc.
225 Arlington Street
Framingham, MA 01702-8723
phone: 1-800-257-5376
fax: 800-268-6624
www.theraproducts.com

17) Vital Links
6613 Seybold Road, Suite E
Madison, WI 53719
phone: 608-270-5424
fax: 1-866-636-9720
www.vitallinks.net

18) Weighted Wearables
1203 Ballentine Rd.
Menomonie, WI 54751
phone: 715-505-3651
fax: 715-309-2268
www.weightedwearables.com

19) Western Psychological Services (WPS)
12031 Wilshire Boulevard
Los Angeles, CA 90025-1251
phone: 1-800-648-8857
fax: 310-478-7838
www.wpspublish.com

LIST OF ADDITIONAL READING

Ayres, A. J. (1979). <u>Sensory integration and the child.</u> Los Angeles, CA: Western Psychological Services.

Dennison, P., & Dennison, G. (1994). <u>Brain Gym Teacher's Edition Revised.</u> Ventura, CA: Edu-Kinesthetics.

Haldy, M., & Haack, L. (1995). <u>Making it easy: Sensorimotor activities at home and school.</u> San Antonio, TX: Therapy Skill Builders.

Joe, B.E. (1998). Are weighted vests worth their weight? <u>OT Week,</u> May 21.

Kerr, T. (1995). How does your engine run? <u>Advance for OT,</u> 11 (9), 12.

Kohl, M.F. (1992). <u>Mudworks: Creative clay, dough, and modeling experiences.</u> Bright Ideas For Learning Centers.

Kranowitz, C. (1998). <u>The out-of-sync child: Recognizing and coping with sensory integration dysfunction.</u> New York, NY: Skylight Press.

Laurel, M. (2000). Bringing sensory integration home: A parent perspective on the alert program for self-regulation. <u>Autism/Asperger's Digest,</u> March-April.

McClanahan, C. (1990). Sensory Integration and hand function: A clinical Perspective. <u>Sensory Integration Special Interest Section Newsletter.</u> Bethesda, MD: American Occupational Therapy Association.

Reisman, J., & Scott, N. (1991). <u>Learning about learning disabilities.</u> San Antonio, TX: Therapy Skill Builders. [Videotape].

Reisman, J. (Executive Producer), & Connors, K. (Director). (1996). <u>Sensory Processing for parents: From roots to wings.</u> [Videotape/DVD]. (Available from: The OT Department at the University of Minnesota, 388MMC, Minneapolis, MN 44544).

Rynaski, H. (1996). How does your engine run? <u>OT Week,</u> 8 (47), 20-22.

Trott, M.A, et al. (1993). <u>SenseAbilities: understanding sensory integration.</u> San Antonio, TX: Therapy Skill Builders.

Turecki, S. (1985). <u>The difficult child.</u> New York: Bantam Books.

Wilbarger, P. (1990). <u>Sensory defensiveness.</u> Hugo, MN: PDP Press, Inc. [Videotape].

Wilbarger, P., & Wilbarger, J. (In press). <u>Sensory defensiveness in children ages two to twelve: an intervention guide for parents and other caretakers.</u> (2nd ed.). Van Nuys, CA: Avanti Educational Programs.

Williams, M. S., & Shellenberger, S. (1994). The alert program for self-regulation. <u>Sensory Integration Special Interest Section Newsletter,</u> Bethesda, MD: American Occupational Therapy Association. 17, (3).

NOTES

NOTES